I0441991

Pioneer
Free Will Baptists
Ministers
Burial Locations
In
North Carolina

ALTON LOVELESS 1

This book was printed in the United States of America.

To order additional copies of this book, contact:
FWB Publications
Enchanting Acres
1006 Rayme Drive
Columbus, Ohio 43207
Alton.loveless@prodigy.net
Or
www.amazon.com

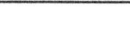

FWB
FWB Publications

Introduction

North Carolina

This book represents all that were part of the Free Will Baptist movement, consisting of the Palmer (south), Randall (north) and others such as the Stone, John-Thomas, John Wheeler Assns., NC OFWB and more.

Many of the photos are poor quality, but it was all I could find. Likewise, I do not have photos or tombstones for many of them. The information about these ministers were all that was available to me or found in archives. I made every effort to include those for which they would be remembered. Some I had no information, but research had shown they were of our denomination

North Carolina

Rev Dennis William Alexander, Sr
Birth:
Oct. 16, 1891
North Carolina
Death:
Jan. 20, 1975
Burial:
Bethel Town Cemetery
Bethel
Pitt County
North Carolina,

An active FWB minister in the Eastern General Association, and registered as minister in their Minutes of meetings.

John William Alford
Birth:
Oct. 3, 1881
Death:

Dec. 5, 1960
Burial:
Kenly Cemetery,
Kenly, Johnston County,
North Carolina

A recognized and respected pastor in eastern North Carolina. Even at age 75 he was driving 100 miles to pastor. He was a brother in law to Mrs. Alice Lupton who was an early leader in the women's movement in North Carolina and on the national level. Records show that he was a member of foreign missions board in the late 50s.

William Edmond Anderson
Birth:
Dec. 9, 1872
North Carolina,
Death:
Feb. 9, 1958
Morehead City
Carteret County
North Carolina
Burial:
Woodlawn Memorial Park
Durham
Durham County
North Carolina

Listed as ordained Free Will Baptist minister in 1916 Western Conference Minutes of Orig. FWB when convened at Johnston Co. NC. His address was "Durham, NC." Age: 85.

Joseph Garfield Ange

Birth:
Dec. 19, 1922
Martin County, North Carolina
Death:
Jul. 16, 2011
Raleigh, Wake County,
North Carolina
Burial:
Win, Washington County,
North Carolina

Ange pastored Free Will Baptist churches in Tennessee, Michigan, and North Carolina. From 1960 to 1976, he served on the Foreign Mission Board for Free Will Baptists. In 1971, Dr. Ange was awarded an Honorary Doctorate from Bob Jones University. In 1972 he became the director of Religious Activities and the Campus Pastor at Free Will Baptist Bible College in Nashville, TN. Dr. Ange was elected the first full-time President of Southeastern Free Will Baptist College in 1983. He oversaw the construction and occupation of the new campus in 1987. As long as his health permitted, Dr. Ange was a devoted member of Landmark Free Will Baptist Church, where he served as an Adult Sunday School teacher and Senior Saints pastor for 10 years.

Dr. Gerald Porter Ballard

Birth:
Oct. 16, 1936
North Carolina
Death:
Mar. 24, 2014
Shell Point Village
Lee County, Florida
Burial:
Cremation

The youngest son of Baptist minister Reverend Loy Everett Ballard and Gertrude Oakley Ballard, Jerry grew up immersed in a strong and deep belief in God. As his faith in God grew, so did his passion to reach out to others in the name of Jesus to empower their lives not only with the gospel but also with provisions for their daily lives. Graduating high school in Ayden, NC, Jerry went on to earn degrees from East Carolina University, Columbia Bible College, and Syracuse University.

When Jerry was little, his family moved from town to town because his father was a circuit minister, so Jerry created his own world complete with close friends. He was fond of telling us how he had a group of imaginary friends. One boy was Chinese, one black African and a third from India. Their favorite game? Shooting marbles. These imaginary friends and those games provided the appreciation for all cultures around the world and laid the foundation for his greatest challenge in life: spearheading the international relief and development arm of the National Association of Evangelicals known as World Relief Corporation from 1978-1991.

Jerry loved and ultimately mastered the power of words—in writing, teaching, and in international negotiation. His first official reporting assignment scooped the landmark case that resulted in passing the law requiring school busses to have side-panel stop signs and flashing red lights, making it illegal for vehicles to pass a stopped school bus while children loaded or unloaded. Of the articles he wrote during the 1950s, he was especially proud of having interviewed a young upcoming actor in 1956 by the name of Andy Griffith.

Jerry and Winnie were long acquainted because of their shared denomination. They finally officially met and started dating when they were teenagers. They married in August 1958 and left eastern North Carolina for Columbia, SC to attend Columbia Bible College. Upon graduation, Jerry and Winnie moved to Nashville, TN to join the Free Will Baptist Foreign Missions Board. Soon their family grew—Kim was born in 1963 and Keri was born in 1967.

Since high school, Jerry wrote prolifically for newspapers, communication as well as marketing and advertising, and several books, winning numerous awards. For Free Will Baptist Foreign Missions Board he created Heartbeat magazine, films and film strips linking the church with missions worldwide. When World Vision International invited him to join their headquarters in Monrovia, CA, he pioneered communication through television and magazine writing and editing as well as raised funds with such innovative projects as the Love Loaf, created by Bobb Biehl.

The Ballard's moved back to the

east coast where Jerry taught in a newly formed Master's Program Communications Department with radio, recording and television studios at Columbia Bible College, now Columbia International University in S.C. Jerry began fielding so many marketing and advertising projects that he opened Jerry Ballard Associates in Atlanta hiring Merriana Branan straight out of art school while Winnie ran the office. Jerry took on as partner his long-time friend and award-winning artist Kent Puckett whose wife Pat took over the billing and finance department for Winnie. Kent and Jerry excelled with highly creative and successful campaigns for Christian and secular organizations with such clients as the Stephen Olford Ministries, Bill Gaither Trio, and Chic-fil-A. In 1977, Dr. Everett Graffam retired as CEO of World Relief Commission (now World Relief Corporation), and Jerry, having been a Board member, was invited to become CEO, providing for people at risk worldwide primarily working through established, national churches and missionaries, including CMA. In the early 1980s, Jerry appointed Grady Mangham from CMA as vice President in charge of refugee resettlement during the war in Cambodia, Vietnam, and Laos setting up a model program for receiving the "boat people" in nations of first asylum and resettling them in participating countries. The writings he

produced during this time were the most brilliant, succinct insights into the human condition and call to meet the needs of people everywhere in the name of Jesus. After Jerry retired from World Relief he continued to work for the causes he loved by consulting with Christian Children's Fund, the Heifer Project, and Feed the Children. He and Don Miltner teamed up for some projects and to write materials for fund raising for a Christian school in Cary, NC before retiring with Winnie to Shell Point in 2006.

Loy Everett Ballard
Birth:
Mar. 20, 1899
Buncombe County, North Carolina
Death:
Nov. 19, 1978 Greenville, Pitt County,
North Carolina
Burial:
Greenwood Cemetery,
Greenville, Pitt County,
North Carolina

He was born in the mountains of Western North Carolina where he spent the majority of his years as a Free Will Baptist ministers within the bounds of the North Carolina State Convention where he served more than 50 years. Not only was his leadership shown as a pastor to the local church, but was very active in organizing the Free Will Baptist League within his area. He also played an active role in establishing and promoting Craigmont Assembly serving 10 years as co-manager with his wife. For 22 years he was Field Sec. of the state Sunday school convention he also served the Free Will Baptist orphanage at Middlesex as director of religious work. He attended Mars Hill College and the Free Will Baptist Seminary in Ayden.

He served pastorates throughout North Carolina as well as holding the state and national offices in the denomination as listed. He was known as an avid collector of memorabilia and gave his valuable historical materials about Free Will Baptists to the Free Will Baptist Historical Collection at Mount Olive College. He also wrote for many of Free Will Baptist denominational publications encouraging the gathering of materials about Free Will Baptist history. He was the father of Dr Gerald Porter Ballard who held many roles in the national convention and also was director of World Relief of the National Association of Evangelicals.

John Henry Ballard
Birth:
Oct. 23, 1844
Yancey County, North Carolina
Death:
Jul. 8, 1934 Walnut, Madison County,
North Carolina
Burial:
Ballard Cemetery,
Buncombe County,
North Carolina

Rev. John H. Ballard was an ordained Free Will Baptist minister, being ordained after 1865. He was converted in Oct. 1862, but served in the Union Army for NC, until it ended. Afterward, the Association wanted him to be ordained and he was reluctant because he had limited education. He preached for over fifty years, and had a fruitful ministry. He was a friend of the Temperance movement and all benevolent causes. The French Broad Association, of which he was affiliated, wrote a tribute they published to honor him and his long life of usefulness in the gospel ministry.

Willis W Ballard
Birth:
1868
Death:
1924
Burial:
Ballard Cemetery, Barnardsville,
Buncombe County,
North Carolina

James Moses Barfield
Birth:
Oct. 13, 1838
Greene County, North Carolina
Death:
Sep. 3, 1918
Burial:
Ayden Cemetery, Ayden,
Pitt County, North Carolina

Co-Author of the Barfield and Harrison History of North Carolina Free Will Baptists. He served as a Confederate soldier under the command of Capt. Byrd and in the battalion commanded by Maj. Harding of Greenville. He was licensed to preach the gospel in the year 1867 and was ordained soon after to the full work of the ministry. He was devoted to the Free Will Baptist Denomination and did all in his power to advance their doctrine which he felt was the doctrine of the Bible. It is said that he was not a brilliant speaker, nor great orator and word painter. He was one of the earliest ministers interested in a publication for the denomination, which was first published in the town of Fremont, but later moved to Elm City in Wilson County. Later the conferences in North Carolina, with the exception of one, took the matter under their consideration and Elder R. H. Hearn was elected editor and ran the paper in new Bern for several years. Later a Elder Barfield became editor and publisher and soon the office was moved to Ayden by the stockholders in 1897. Elder Barfield was also a pioneer in the work of the Seminary which was started shortly after he moved to Ayden while publishing the *Free Will Baptists,* the state publication.

Jesse Parrott Barrow
Birth:
Oct. 26, 1898
Greene County, North Carolina
Death:
Mar. 11, 1990
Nashville, Davidson County, Tennessee
Burial:
Hull Road Church Cemetery, Greene County, North Carolina
Rev. Jesse P. was student at the Free Will Baptist Seminary, Ayden, NC, per his 1917 WW I Draft Registration. In 1920, he was employed in Chicago, perhaps

where he met Anna, his future wife. He possibly studied at a College in Nashville, where they were living in 1945-46, per old minutes which stated Nashville as their residence. In the 1949 Nashville City Directory, he and Anna were still in Nashville, with "Free Will Bible College." The 1958 Nashville City Directory showed him employed as Teacher at FWBBC, and Anna as Librarian there. Records show Rev. J. P. Barrow as having served on National FWB Church Boards and committees. He was honored as a leader and minister among the church.

Nigel Bruce Barrow
Birth:
October 23, 1911
Greene County, North Carolina
Death:
March 8, 2004
Greene County, North Carolina
Burial:
Hull Road Church Cemetery, Greene County, North Carolina

Rev J A Blalock
Birth:
Mar. 22, 1869
Death:
Oct. 7, 1960
Burial:
Greenwood Cemetery
Dunn
Harnett County
North Carolina

An ordained minister of the Free Will Baptist church, whose name is in list of ministers in 1903, Conference, in Harnett Co. N.C. when meeting at the Hodges Chapel Church.

Thomas Elijah Beaman
Birth:
Jan. 6, 1899
North Carolina
Death:
Dec. 7, 1961
Goldsboro,
Wayne County, North Carolina
Burial:
Willow Dale Cemetery,
Goldsboro,
Wayne County, North Carolina

Well-known Free Will Baptist minister in North Carolina and the National Convention in the 50's and 60's, he attended Moody Bible Institute and Northwestern Theological Seminary in Chicago and later attended the graduate school at Texas A&M University. He was ordained to the ministry in 1931 at the Hull Road Original Free Will Baptist Church. He was faithful to his ministry over seven decades and during this period pastored over 30 churches, principally in Eastern North Carolina. He served as the Assistant Superintendent of the Children's Home at Middlesex and was a founding member of the Board of Trustees of Mount Olive College. He managed the denomination's publishing house in Ayden during the 1960s. His family established the Barrow Family Endowment at Mount Olive College endowing professorship in the Department of Religion

Jesse R Bennett
Birth:
Jul. 1, 1902
Death:
Jan. 17, 1964
Burial:
New Bern Memorial Cemetery,
Trent Woods,
Craven County, North Carolina,
Plot: Section A

Rev Edward Dee Bissette
Birth:
Feb. 1, 1890
Nash County
North Carolina,
Death:
Apr. 9, 1970
Nash County
North Carolina
Burial:

Bailey Cemetery
Bailey
Nash County
North Carolina

Rev Edward Dee Bissette; son of Kennon and Etta Bailey Bissette Rev. Dee Bissette," is listed in a roll of ordained Free Will Baptist ministers in 1935 Minutes of the Western Conference of Free Will Baptist, which included Nash, Wilson, and other counties.

Rev. Dee Bissette, is also shown in several obits in Wilson Co. *Daily Times*, as having conducted funerals for Free Will Baptist persons at the White Oak FWB Church, Wilson County, in the 1940's and on up through the 1960's.

Andrew Jackson Bordeaux
Birth:
May 17, 1840
New Hanover County
North Carolina, USA
Death:
Aug. 1, 1916

Bladen County
North Carolina
Burial:
Haw Bluff Baptist Church
Cemetery
Kelly
Bladen County
North Carolina

An active minister in the early history of the Free Will Baptist church, and his name appearing in old church records. Son of Rebecca Holly and James Bordeaux.
Enlisted in Company A, North Carolina Co. A 1st Heavy Artillery Company on 15 May 1862.Promoted to Full Corporal on 08 Aug 1863.

Clarence F. Bowen
Birth:
January 5, 1912
Death:
January 22, 1984
Wayne County, North Carolina
Burial:
Stoney Creek, Stoney Creek,

Wayne County, North Carolina

He was a well-known pastor, writer, and denominational leader for the FWB League. He was a past president of the North Carolina state convention and had been honored as Minister Of The Year by the convention. He was a graduate of Campbell and Wake Forest universities. He received his master's degree at George Peabody College For Teachers in Nashville, Tennessee. He was the pastor of the Pleasant Hill, First Free Will Baptist Church of Wilson, and Stony Creek Free Will Baptist Churches in N.C. He also had served as pastor of the East Nashville Free Will Baptist Church in Nashville, Tennessee. He was an honorary life member of the North Carolina Free Will Baptist Foreign Mission Board and had for many years been a writer for the Free Will Baptist Church Literature Program.

William G. Boykin
Birth:
Oct. 10, 1900
Death:
Mar. 1, 1974
Burial:
Raines Crossroads
Cemetery
Princeton
Johnston County,
North Carolina

An ordained Free Will Baptist minister, whose name appears in early NC records, minutes, etc.

Charles Brown
Birth:
Unknown
Death:
Feb. 22, 1998
Goldsboro, Wayne County,
North Carolina
Burial:
Evergreen Memorial Cemetery,
Goldsboro,
Wayne, North Carolina

Levi Braxton
Birth:
Nov. 7, 1886
Death:
Oct. 15, 1964
Burial:
Hollywood Cemetery
Farmville
Pitt County, North Carolina

Early North Carolina FWB minister.

He had a fruitful ministry of 42 years out of his life of 75. He organized seven churches in three states which included North Carolina, South Carolina and Virginia. His most noted work was the Collingswood Free Will Baptist Church in Portsmouth, Virginia where he pastored 13 years. He also started two other churches in the Tidewater Virginia area. The Great Bridge and Faith Free Will Baptist churches.

Noah D. Brown
Birth:
July 8, 1918
Death:
February 8, 1988
Burial:
Mount Moriah Cemetery, Garner, Wake County, North Carolina

Seldon D. Bullard
Birth:
Unknown
Death:
Sep. 26,
Myrtle Beach,
Horry County, South Carolina
Burial:
Guilford Memorial Park,
Greensboro,
Guilford County, North Carolina

He was a native of Carthage, North Carolina, but moved to Myrtle Beach, South Carolina in 1970 and organized the First Free Will Baptist Church. He had served pastorates in Darlington, South Carolina; Louisa, Kentucky; Bristol, Tennessee; Glennville, Georgia; Leadington, Missouri; and Morehead city, North Carolina. He

received his theological training at Columbia Bible College. He was an active denominational leader serving on the General Board of the National Association of Free Will Baptists, Superintendent of the Kentucky Children's Orphanage in Louisa, Kentucky, and on the National Publications Board.

Tommy Lynn Burch, Jr
Birth:
unknown
Death:
Oct. 26, 2012
Bryson City, Swain County, North Carolina
Burial:
Cornerstone Wesleyan Church Cemetery, Bryson City, Swain County, North Carolina

A native of Tennessee, Tommy spent over 30 years of his life in Graham and Swain Counties. He was a Minister and Pastored Churches in Elizabethton TN at Moore's Chapel Freewill Baptist Church and in Bryson City at Sawmill Hill Freewill Baptist Church. He graduated from The Freewill Baptist Bible College) with a B.S. degree in Pastoral Administration and also an E.T.T.A. Teaching diploma. He also worked for Swain County West Elementary School for 12 years.

J. W. Byrd
Birth:
Aug. 30, 1867
Death:
Sep. 7, 1917
Burial:
Saint Mary's Grove Original
Free Will BC Cemetery,
Benson, Johnston County,
North Carolina

Rev Ruffin Bryant Carroll
Birth:
Oct. 10, 1864
North Carolina
Death:
Sep. 24, 1940
Bailey

Nash County
North Carolina
Burial:
Rock Springs Free Will Baptist
Church Cemetery
Bailey
Nash County
North Carolina
An ordained Free Will Baptist minister/pastor.

J F Casey
Birth:
Sep. 30, 1872
Death:
Dec. 31, 1918
Burial:
Willow Dale Cemetery,
Goldsboro
Wayne County, North Carolina

Mance R. Cason
Birth:
Unknown
Death:
Jun. 22, 2016
Morehead City

Carteret County
North Carolina
Burial:
Gethsemane Memorial Park
Morehead City
Carteret County
North Carolina

Dr. Mance R. Cason, 88, of Morehead City, NC passed away at his home. A funeral service was held at First Free Will Baptist Church in Morehead City with Rev. Rick Cason and Rev. Reuben Cason officiating. Dr. Cason was a pastor for over 68 years; for 20 of those years he served at First Free Will Baptist Church in Morehead City.

Rev James W Chatham
Birth:
Jan., 1849
Alexander County
North Carolina
Death:
1925
Morganton
Burke County
North Carolina
Burial:
Broughton Hospital Cemetery
Morganton
Burke County
North Carolina, Plot: r26 g8

James W Chatham is the son of Joseph Maxwell Chatham and Martha Artela Underwood. He was reared in Alexander County, NC and is a brother to Sarah Jane, Mary E, Rachel Amanda and Joseph Elisha Maxwell Chatham.

Named in Woolsey's Hist. as a minister in the Freewill Baptist, who were in the John Wheeler Association organized in 1881, in Washington, Co. VA. (Washington Co. and NC's Sullivan Co. were next to each other, in NC's eastern part, next to VA. This Association was an outgrowth of the Toe River Association in Sullivan Co. TN.

According to online family trees James is said to have had a traumatic brain injury and to have served as a clergyman. He was admitted to the asylum after 1910.

Floyd B. Cherry
Birth:
April 15, 1916
Dothan, Alabama
Death:
February 24, 2005
North Carolina
Burial:
Selma Memorial Gardens,
Selma,
Johnston County,
North Carolina

He was an educator, minister, and writer in the Free Will Baptist denomination. Dr. Cherry, was a native of Alabama and was a minister for 65 years beginning at the age of 16. He was ordained a Free Will Baptist minister in Dothan, Alabama on July 16, 1933. He pastored churches in Alabama, Florida, Georgia and North Carolina. He attended Zion Bible School in Georgia; the University of Florida where he received a bachelor's degree in Bible Study; and Thomas Edison College, where he received his Master's in Bible Study. He earned his Doctor's Degree from Bob Jones University in Greenville, South Carolina in 1975. He came to pastor the Pine Level Free Will Baptist Church in North Carolina where he was the founder of the Carolina Bible Institute that still continues to this day. He wrote three books and also several pamphlets..

Rev Carey Cheshire
BIRTH
22 Jul 1924
Bladen County, North Carolina, USA
DEATH
13 Feb 1992 (aged 67)
Greenville, Pitt County, North Carolina, USA
BURIAL
Westview Cemetery
Kinston, Lenoir County, North Carolina, USA

Carey was the son of Edward Cheshire and his wife Sarah Guyton. He was the grandson of Lydia Graves and Richard J Cheshire of Bladen County, NC. He was the husband of Teachie Edwards. FWBapt minister and pastor.

Rev Cadmus Hunter Coates
Birth:
Apr. 16, 1899
Death:
Aug. 13, 1968
Burial:
Lakeside Memorial Gardens
Angier
Harnett County
North Carolina

He was an Original Free Will Baptist minister active in the formation of the North Carolina State Association of Orig. FWB.

Richard Ray Cordell
Birth:
Aug. 28, 1935
Cincinnati, Ohio,
Death:
Jul. 28, 2011
Goldsboro, North Carolina
Burial:
Evergreen Memorial Cemetery,
Goldsboro,
Wayne County, North Carolina

He served his Lord in ministry for over 54 years and had also served his country in the United States Army. Pastor Cordell was a graduate of the Free Will Baptist College in Nashville, Tennessee, where he received a Bachelor of Science degree in Pastoral Studies. His three pastorates included three states: Indiana, Tennessee, and Alabama. After retiring in Guin, Alabama, Rev. Cordell served for three years as the promotional director for the Alabama Free Will Baptist State Association. He later came to Goldsboro to serve as the Outreach Pastor for Faith Free Will Baptist Church. His greatest joy in

W. Ruffin Coats
Birth:
Dec. 2, 1866
Death:
Sep. 11, 1950
Burial:
Saint Mary's Grove Original
Free Will Baptist church Cemetery
Benson, Johnston County,
North Carolina

life was door-knocking, leading someone to the Lord and asking people to come and visit the church.

Louis N Coscia
Birth:
1926
Death:
May 23, 2010
Burial:
West Memorial Park,
Weaverville,
Buncombe County,
North Carolina

A native of Memphis, Tenn., Rev. Coscia was a Free Will Baptist Missionary serving for 28 years in Brazil. Louis was a running and jogging enthusiast and a gardener. He especially enjoyed growing pansies and is known by many in his area as the "pansy man." He enjoyed reading and writing poetry and had a wonderful sense of humor. A celebration of Rev. Coscia's life was held with Rev. Danny Gasperson officiating.

The will of the One who understands.

Clyde W. Cox
Birth:
Mar. 26, 1920
Rowan County, North Carolina
Death:
Unknown
Wilson, Wilson County,
North Carolina
Burial:
Selma Memorial Gardens,
Selma, Johnston County,
North Carolina,

Rev. Cox dedicated his life to the Lord. Throughout his ministry, he was a pastor at 15 churches beginning in 1952 and ending in 2003 at Spring Hill Church in Goldsboro, N.C. He conducted 274 revivals. He also taught music school in churches throughout North Carolina. He sang, played piano, wrote music and songs and directed music for several revivals. Rev. Cox touched many people's lives over the last 52 years as a dedicated messenger of God. He also served in WWII in the US Navy on the USS Birmingham in the Pacific.

The Refreshing Of The Soul In The Presence Of Jesus.

Rev M E Cox
Birth:
May 20, 1927
Bath
Beaufort County
North Carolina
Death:
Jul. 7, 2016

North Carolina
Burial: [Edit]
Oakdale Cemetery
Washington
Beaufort County
North Carolina

He was born in Bath where he graduated from high school May 10, 1944. He was a World War II Veteran. Rev. Cox spent most of his life in the ministry of Original Free Will Baptist. He served in several capacities including 18 years as moderator of the Piedmont Conference and in several churches as pastor and was originally ordained in July 1956. He was the author of the book "From the Plow to the Pulpit."

John S. Craft
Birth:
1942
North Carolina
Death:
1980

Burial:
Ayden Cemetery, Ayden,
Pitt County, North Carolina

He was a Free Will Baptist missionary serving in Brazil from 1968-1973.

Today is not a day of distress
But a day of delight.

Elder Parrot Creech
Birth:
Sep. 12, 1832
Death:
Jan. 6, 1874
Burial:
Saint Mary's Grove Original Free Will Baptist Cemetery,
Benson,
Johnston County, North Carolina

Elder Creech was founder of St. Mary's Grove Original Free Will Baptists Church

John Linward Crocker, Sr
Birth:
Apr. 1, 1931
Death:
Dec. 12, 2010
Burial:
Branch Chapel Free Will Baptist Church,
Smithfield,
Johnston County, North Carolina

Funeral services at Branch Chapel Free Will Baptist Church with the Rev. Terry Dennis and Mr. Luby Tyner officiating. Burial was with military honors.

Elder Moses LaFlaver Cummings
Birth:
Jun. 2, 1876
Canada
Death:
Dec. 26, 1963
Raleigh
Wake County
North Carolina
Burial:

Marsh Swamp Church Cemetery
Wilson
Wilson County
North Carolina

Son of Richard Cummings and Cordelia Pickens. FindaGrave contributor Winnie shared that "he was an ordained minister in the Free Will Baptist church, shown in 1935 Minutes' list of ministers in the Western Conference".

Inscription:
Traveling Evangelist and Home Missionary

Known as "Blackie of the North Woods"

Rev William Alonzo Dail
Birth:
Aug. 22, 1876
Pitt County
North Carolina
Death:
Jan. 1, 1956
Pitt County
North Carolina
Burial:
Reedy Branch Baptist Church Cemetery
Winterville
Pitt County, North Carolina

Rev. William A. Dail was the son of Thomas Dail and Sarah (Cannon) DAIL. He died at aged 79 yrs, having lived most of his life in the Winterville area. He was an ordained Free Will Baptist minister. He served several churches as pastor in counties in northeastern North Carolina, before failing health caused him to retire about ten years prior to his death. He married Hattie L. Barber.

The deacons of Reedy Branch Free Will Baptist Church served as pallbearers, and members of the FWB Central Conference were honorary bearers.

Frank Davenport

Birth:
1923
Death:
1997
Goldsboro,
Wayne County, North Carolina
Burial:
Wayne Memorial Park,
Goldsboro,
Wayne County, North Carolina

He was a Church builder organizing 12 churches in North Carolina where he spent most of his ministry. He also helped start four Christian schools. All were in North Carolina. His longest pastorate was a 20 year tenure at the Faith Free Will Baptist church in Goldsboro, one of the 12 churches he organized. His ministry spanned 45 years in North Carolina and Kentucky.

He was a native of Pitt County, North Carolina. He was ordained to preach in 1952 at age 29. As a leader he was elected to numerous positions in North Carolina and on the national level.

He served six years on the national Home Mission Board and on the national Executive Committee. He Served The North Carolina State Home Missions, and the Bible Bookstore Board.

He was also manager of Jubilee, Inc. and as Treasurer of the Free Will Baptist Superannuation Assn.

Rev Arthur Lee Davidson

BIRTH
2 Jul 1892
Georgia, USA
DEATH
14 Jan 1938 (aged 45)
Greenville, Pitt County, North Carolina, USA
BURIAL
Winterville Cemetery
Winterville, Pitt County, North Carolina, USA
PLOT   Section 2

Arthur and Daisy were the parents of: Annie Ruth Davidson Nobles, Elbert Lee Davidson, Myra Nell

Davidson Rouse Nada Davidson Tripp and Dr. William Franklin Davison (7 Jan 1936)

Arthur Lee Davidson began an active Christian life at the age of 18 as a member of the Free Will Baptist Church. He became ordained to preach his ministry and pastored in Georgia, Alabama, North Carolina and South Carolina. An ordained Free Will Baptist minister, who was in the formation of the eastern and western churches into the National Association of FWB. His notice of death was in the 1938 Minutes of National.

James Robert Davidson
Birth:
May 28, 1898
Death:
Jan. 9, 1972
Burial:
New Bern Memorial Cemetery,
Trent Woods,
Craven County, North Carolina,
Plot: Section G

Davison is remembered as a long-time crusader for Christian education. Davison made the Board Of Education's report at the 1939 session of the national Association at Bryan, Texas with the proposition of beginning a national Bible college. He at the 1942 meeting in Columbus, Mississippi during his report for that the board was authorized by the convention to open the school in Nashville, Tennessee on September 15, 1942. The first building purchased by the college still bears the name of the man who labored for the college's promotion for so many years. He served on the Board of Trustees of the college in 1943 until 1964. During this 21 year tenure, he served as chairman, vice chairman, and secretary of the board. He also served the as Business Manager during 1942-1944 and again in 1946-1947 He served the National Association as an Assistant Moderator from 1938-1944. At the 1940 for meeting he was elected as Moderator, a post he held until 1946.

Rev James E Davis
Birth:
Dec. 5, 1918
Death:
Apr. 26, 2006
urial:
Ashelawn Gardens of Memory
Asheville
Buncombe County
North Carolina

Rev J.E. Davis' name was in roll of ordained ministers in the 1935 Western Conference Minutes.

Benjamin Bardin Deans
Birth:
Mar. 18, 1866
Death:
Jun. 17, 1934
Burial:
Joseph J. Bissette Cemetery,
Nash County,
North Carolina

Garrett Deweese
Birth:
1772
Botetourt County,
Virginia
Death:
Nov. 28, 1839
Buncombe County,
North Carolina

Burial:
Big Ivy Cemetery,
Barnardsville,
Buncombe County,
North Carolina

He was the son of Henry Deweese and Elizabeth (Hughes) Deweese, both bn PA. (per Family Trees).

He married Susannah Palmer about 1795 in Buncombe, NC. They had nine children.

He was an early Baptist preacher, but became of the free will type, and worked in North Carolina and East Tennessee region with Revs Moses Peterson and John Wheeler. At first they were members of the French Broad Association of Baptists. This Association became divided over the Calvinistic and the Arminian question. The Arminian group led by Rev. Garrett Deweese, was "free will" but practiced close communion. Although the Reverends Peterson and Wheeler agreed with Deweese on the question of the free moral agency of man and they both invited all Christians to the Communion, they agreed to meet with prayer, and settle the questions between them regarding communion. They did that became known as the "Free Will Baptist." Pioneers from other parts of North Carolina and Virginia settled here, which were of this persuasion, and six small churches were formed, in five counties, in two states, and separated by mountains. These old preachers carried out their "calling" in very difficult circumstances and hardships.

A little later, Rev. Wm. Bonaparte WOOLSEY, joined in and formed the Toe River Association of Free Will Bapt. churches which during his lifetime, grew tremendously.

Not many records exists of Rev. Deweese's detailed ministry, but the records do show he was a faithful man and a leader in his time for his Free Will Baptist church to help serve the spiritual needs of these scattered people.

His son, Levi, also became a minister.

Where he is buried is not exactly known, as I have found no records that show where he was interred. Rev. Garrett Dewesse, and first wife, Susanna Palmer Deweese, lived in Buncombe and died there...she in 1815-16, and he in 1839, and his Will was proved in January, 1840, Buncombe Co. NC.

I've been told there are no "Deweese" family buried in Big Ivy Cemetery; it is recorded that Deweese preached at that Baptist church, and may have pastored it.

Levi Deweese
Birth:
Sep. 2, 1810
North Carolina
Death:
May 25, 1902
North Carolina
Burial:
Gabriels Creek Baptist Church,
Cemetery,
Mars Hill, Madison County,
North Carolina

Rev. Levi Deweese was the son of Rev. Garrett and Susannah (Palmer) Deweese..In the Census of 1850, Levi was listed as a head of household in Buncombe Co, NC. .A pioneer Free Will Baptist preacher in North Carolina and East Tennessee..

Sigbee Bryant Dilda
Birth:
Jan. 8, 1936
Death:
Sep. 11, 2002
Greenville
Pitt County, North Carolina
Burial:
Queen Anne Cemetery
Fountain
Pitt County, North Carolina

Rev Sigbee Dilda, former pastor of Pamplico FWB Church, NAFWB General Board member from South Carolina for many years, and longtime soldier of the Cross went to be with the Lord on September 11th. Brother Sigbee had recently resigned from Pamplico FWB Church and moved to Hookerton,NC because of ill health.

His wife, Mary, had taught for many years at Maranatha Christian School (First FWB Church, Florence) and is now continuing her labors at Mt. Calvary Christian School; where she lives close to son, Bryant. Daughter, Susanna, is married to Rev Carroll Bazen,Pastor of Grace FWB Church in Lake City, SC.Many things stand out about Brother Sigbee. He was a long time Pastor Glenwood FWB Church (Arkansas) 1965-67; Pamplico FWB Church (SC) 1967-1970; Ruth's Chapel FWB Church (NC) 1970-1980; Great Bridge FWB Church (Virginia) 1980-1983; Tabernacle FWB Church (NC) 1983-89; Lebanon FWB Church (SC) 1989-1990; Pamplico FWB Church (SC) 1990-2002. He believed what he believed and was willing to stand for that belief (A sentiment echoed by all of the speakers at his funeral service). He knew how to have fun but he also knew when to stand firm. And he was a faithful soul winner and soldier for the Lord.

Rev Burrell Thomas Dixon
Birth:
May 5, 1870
Death:
Feb. 16, 1951
Burial:
Pineview Cemetery
South Rocky Mount
Edgecombe County
North Carolina
Plot: PV: 46:0:86

Ordained Free Will Bapt. minister/pastor in NC. Name on roll of Western Conference minutes in 1935.

Robert Jefferson Durham
Birth:
Mar. 23, 1927
Wayne County, North Carolina
Death:
Sep. 9, 2012
Rocky Mount, Nash County, North Carolina
Burial:
Rocky Mount Memorial Park, Rocky Mount
Nash County, North Carolina

He was born in Wayne County to the late Jeff and Pearl Harris Durham. He lived with his parents and helped them run their farm until 1945, when he was drafted into the Army. After being stationed in France and completing his service he returned home and worked as a Deputy Sheriff in Greene County.

He later became Associate Sales Manager with the Western and Southern Life Insurance Company where he worked for eleven years, which moved him to Rocky Mount in 1954; during which time he answered the call to preach. He attended the Evangelical Baptist College and graduated from the William Carter Bible College. In 1960, he founded and organized Grace Free Baptist Church with eleven charter members. Prior to his retirement he saw the church attendance grow to over 500, and in 1976 the church founded Grace Christian School. He had a passion for soul winning and preaching God's word and was honored to see ten of the church members be ordained and begin full-time work for God. Reverend Durham was speaker on the Grace Baptist Hour on WECE radio for 20 years. He served two terms as local moderator and six years as state moderator of the Palmer Association of Free Baptist Churches. After retirement, he held numerous revivals, was interim pastor for several area Baptist churches and continued being a faithful working member of Grace Free Baptist Church. He was survived by his devoted loving wife of 63 years, Gladys Speight Durham.

Nathan Earl Eason
Birth:
Nov. 2, 1932
Greene County, North Carolina
Death:
Apr. 4, 2008
Rocky Mount
Nash County, North Carolina
Burial:
Queen Anne Cemetery
Fountain
Pitt County, North Carolina

Nathan Eason married Mary Agnes Dilda on May 24, 1952 in Greenville, Pitt Co., and NC. His parents were James C Eason (1893 - 1975) and Ora Mae Moore Eason (1899 - 1970). He had been the pastor of Grace Free Will Baptist Church in Greenville.

Lonne R. Ennis
Birth:
1895
Death:
1977
Goldsboro,
Wayne County, North Carolina
Burial:
Willow Dale Cemetery,
Goldsboro,
Wayne County, North Carolina

Denominational leader, pastor, educator, and conference speaker. He pioneered for a educational program which was greatly needed in our denomination. The Lord equipped to deal with the keen mind and thorough education he acquired abilities that few men among us possessed.. At a time when we needed an educational vision, and someone who could implement that vision, brother Ennis conducted Bible institutes across our denomination. He built an interest in education which finally resulted in Free Will Baptist Bible College being established in Nashville, Tennessee. He stepped into a world of national prominence among Free Will Baptists in 1940 when he preached the opening sermon in the fourth annual session in Paintsville, Kentucky. His sermon *Rivers Of Living Waters* was considered a masterpiece. He was elected as the first executive Sec. of the restless, newly organized denomination in 1940. He served in that position until 1943. He traveled thousands of miles promoting denomination outreach during which time he. Pastored three churches at the same time and in addition to his extensive travels. He was summons to Nashville, Tennessee in 1944 where he was appointed president of the Free Will Baptist Bible College serving from 1944 until 1947. His training had been secured from Moody Bible Institute and his diplomatic skills required as an Executive Sec. had been soundly tested for the job. He led the college in purchasing the Sword building in 1945, the same year that the college yearbook, *The Lumen* was dedicated to him. He taught a variety of courses while at the college including English, Sunday School and Church Administration, Bible and others. Ennis remained a guiding voice in his native North Carolina because of his great spiritual strength and wisdom.. He was pastoring two churches at his death at age 81. One of the buildings at Free Will Baptist Bible College is named for him.

James A. Evans
Birth:
November 10, 1905
Death:
October 25, 1999
Lucama, Wilson County,
North Carolina
Burial:
Lucas Cemetery, Lucama,
Wilson County, North Carolina

He was a early Free Will Baptist preacher from Wayne County in eastern North Carolina. He attended Eureka College in Ayden,

North Carolina, and was a graduate of the Pastor's Institute of Duke University. In 1994 he received the first honorary Doctor Of Divinity degree given by Mount Olive College. He was an ordained minister for 74 years and served churches in North Carolina, Texas, and Florida. He was selected the outstanding Free Will Baptist Minister of the Year by the North Carolina Association OFWB in 1972. He was the first full-time employee of Mount Olive College where he began in 1954 serving as the Director Of Public Relations. From 1940-1949 he served as the Superintendent of the Children's Home in Middlesex. He was the co-founder of the Free Will Baptist Church Finance Association in 1940 and the first Chairman of Craigmont Assembly of the Original Free Will Baptist Conference Center in 1945.

Rev Orvin B Everett, Sr
BIRTH
19 Sep 1915
DEATH
21 Oct 1993 (aged 78)
BURIAL
Onslow Memorial Park
Jacksonville, Onslow County,
North Carolina, USA

Ordained Original Free Will Baptist minister and pastor. Served churches in North Carolina.

W. B. Everett
Birth:
1877
Death:
1948
Craven County, North Carolina
Burial:
Cedar Grove Cemetery,
New Bern,
Craven County, North Carolina

Early leader and minister in the eastern area of North Carolina. Early leader and minister in the eastern area of North Carolina. He preached at the 1938 session.

James W Everton
Birth:
Nov. 2, 1923
Death:
Mar. 4, 1971
Burial:
East Duplin Memorial Gardens,
Beulaville,
Duplin County, North Carolina

Free Will Baptist preacher and WWII veteran.
Inscription:
GM3 USNR WWII

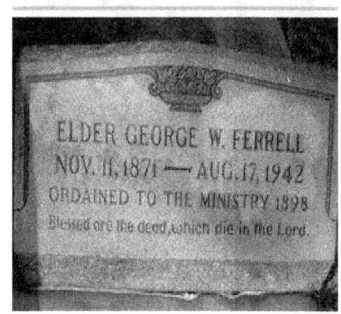

Elder George W. Ferrell
Birth:
Nov. 11, 1871
Wilson, North Carolina
Death:
Aug. 17, 1942
Wilson, North Carolina
Burial:
Stony Hill Free Will Baptist Church Cemetery

Nash County
North Carolina

George is the son of Jacob M. Ferrell and Mary Della Lancaster. He married Martha Bryant. Ordained Free Will Baptist minister listed in minutes of the 1935 Western Conference of Orig. FWB. Active minister and pastor as long as physically able...he was included in the 'retired minister' list at the 1935 session.

William M Ferrell
Birth:
Oct. 25, 1886
Johnston County,
North Carolina
Death:
Nov. 6, 1937
Durham,
Durham County,
North Carolina

Burial:
Bethel Original
Freewill Baptist Church Cemetery,
Four Oaks,
Johnston County,
North Carolina

Rev Zalpheus P. Ferrell
Birth:
Feb. 13, 1857
Death:
May 11, 1940
Burial:
Shady Grove Free Will Baptist
Church Cemetery
Durham
Durham County
North Carolina

His first name was Zalpheus; He used initials, Rev. Z.P.Ferrell. An ordained Free Will Baptist minister/pastor. His name was in list of ministers in Minutes of the 49th Session of the Western Conference, convened in 1935.

Rev Henry Franklin Flowers
Birth:
Nov. 2, 1938
Johnston County
North Carolina
Death:
Nov. 24, 2017
Wayne County
North Carolina
Burial:
Kirby Family Cemetery
Kenly
Johnston County
North Carolina

Frank was born to the late Henry Nathaniel Flowers and Nina Peacock Flowers. He proudly served his country in the United States Army and later attended Edwards Military Institute. Frank also attended Elkins School of Electronics where he received his Federal Communications license. Frank came to Goldsboro in 1968 and started Southern Communications where he owned and operated this company until his retirement in 2000. During his communications career, Frank was instrumental in developing a relationship with the Wayne County Fireman's Association.

Frank received salvation at an early age and answered the call into ministry with the Original Free Will Baptist Church in 1970. He was ordained to preach the gospel in 1971. He gave all of his adult life to the Free Will Baptist denomination, serving twice as pastor of Jackson Heights Free Will Baptist Church and later as pastor of Little Creek Free Will Baptist Church for 26 years. Following his retirement from ministry, Frank continued to serve as an interim pastor for several Free Will Baptist Churches and was a much called upon revival speaker. He also continued to teach at Carolina Bible Institute as well as lead numerous bible studies on Revelations. Frank was active in numerous denominational organizations, as well as serving on the Board of Directors for the Free Will Baptist Press and the Carolina Bible Institute.

He was adored by his family, for whom he was a source of joy and strength, but also by countless others, from old friends to new acquaintances, all of whom were struck by his quiet generosity, his kind and unassuming intelligence, and his innate courteousness.

John Eugene Floyd
Birth:
Jan. 17, 1906
Caldwell County,
North Carolina
Death:
Nov. 21, 1996
Charlotte
Mecklenburg County
North Carolina
Burial:
Hillcrest Gardens
Mount Holly
Gaston County
, North Carolina

Rev. John Floyd, 90, of Mt. Holly, a retired Free Will Baptist pastor, evangelist and church planter. He was converted on July 10, 1927 and was ordained in 1946. He overcame tuberculosis at the age of 24, but still refuse to preach. He struggled to accept the call to preach for 15 years because of his fear and an inability to read and his lack of formal education. Six years later at age 30 after over hearing a doctor tell his wife that he would die of pneumonia, he finally accepted the call. He pastored the First Free Will Baptist Church, Marion, North Carolina in 1946 leading the church to grow from 29 members to 412. He pastored several other churches in the 50s and 60s including the Sea Level and Cedar Island Free Will Baptist churches, and the Calvary Free Will Baptist Church in Jacksonville. At the age of 66 he began pastoring the Adawolfe Free Will Baptist Church in Virginia. The church grew from 60 in Sunday school and added 130 members while baptizing 100 members and had four men call to preach and they paid for a new parsonage. He was known as a man of prayer and prayed that 100 men would enter the ministry through his preaching. Some 132 men did answer the call to preach including his son, a son-in-law, two grandsons and a nephew. Also, through his ministry Miss Volena Wilson went to India as a missionary. He preached in 37 states, Canada, Mexico, Puerto Rico and Jerusalem. He organized 15 churches and preached revivals in 100 churches where he witnessed more than 23,000 professions of faith in response to his 7500 sermons which he preached. He also had a continuing the radio ministry for 30 years.

Elder Frederick Asa Fonville
Birth:
Mar. 6, 1770
Alamance County, North Carolina
Death:
Apr. 21, 1835
Alamance County, North Carolina
Burial:
Fonville Family Cemetery
Alamance County, North Carolina

A pioneer Free Will Baptist minister, along with others, who ministered in the remnant left of the Philadelphia Association, in 1832. He was a worthy and faithful man, of good reputation, who stood on his convictions. Beloved son of Stephen Fonville and Lucy Kibble. He was the husband of Rebecca Oliver, whom he married Jan 29, 1790. Their son was William Washington Fonville. After her death in 1793, he married Mary Polly Averett on Dec 12, 1793. Their children were Nathan Fonville; Hannah Fonville; Edna Fonville; John Averett Fonville; Sallie Fonville; and James Roney Fonville. After Mary died in 1816, he married Charity Graham on May 30, 1816 in Orange, North Carolina. Their children were Mary Fonville; Frederick W Fonville; Asa Graham Fonville; Francis Fonville; and Brice Frederick Fonville. Spouses: Mary Polly Everette Fonville (1775 - 1816). Rebecca Oliver Fonville (1777 -93), -Charity Graham Fonville (1789 - 1858).

William M Fulcher, Jr
Birth:
May 6, 1933
Bridgeton,
Craven County, North Carolina
Death:
Mar. 23, 2004
New Bern,
Craven County, North Carolina
Burial:
Dixon Cemetery, Aurora,
Beaufort County, North Carolina

Bill graduated from the Bridgeton High School in 1952 and thereafter, played baseball for the New Bears. He was drafted into the United States Army in 1953 and served in Korea and Japan. He was trained in radio communication. In 1955 he was honorably discharged from the Army and enrolled in Free Will Baptist Bible College in Nashville Tennessee, to prepare for the Ministry. He graduated in 1959 with a BA degree. While in school he married Linda Barks in 1957 and during their marriage life they had five children. He pastored the Bethany Free Will Baptist Church in Winterville, North Carolina during 1959-1960. It was at the end of 1960 that he was commissioned as a foreign missionary for the International Mission Board Of Free Will Baptists. He attended the Spanish language Institute in San Jose, Costa Rica during 1961. From 1961 to 1969 he served in Uruguay, South America and from 1971 through 1979 served in Panama, Central America. He returned to the pastorate in 1979 and served the Bethel Free Will Baptist Church in S. Roxana, Illinois. He served there until 1981 when He was hired by the National Home Mission Board to serve the Spanish-speaking people in Houston, Texas. In 1988 through 1992 he was employed by the Southeastern Free Will Baptist College in Wendell, North Carolina as the Promotional Director. Afterwards he pastored the Faith Free Will Baptist Church in Carrollton, Virginia from 1992 to 2000, and then the Faith Free Will Baptist Church in Maysville, North Carolina from 2000 until 2004 where he was serving when he died.

Houston Owen Ganey

Birth:
Nov. 17, 1931
Death:
Mar. 23, 2003
Nashville, Davidson County,
Tennessee
Burial:
Richmond Memorial Park,
Rockingham, Richmond County,
North Carolina

Brother Ganey was a well-respected minister, evangelist and pastor. He was always an encourager to all who knew him. The native North Carolinian was living in Nashville at the time of his death.

Owen B. Garriss

Birth:
Nov. 12, 1850
Death:
Sep. 11, 1929
Burial:
Garriss Cemetery (Watha)
Pender County, North Carolina

Son of Rufus & Sophia J. Garriss. His name was listed in 1903 Harnett Co. NC Free Will Baptist roll of ministers.

Rev Henry Hood Goff
Birth:
1874
Death:
1950
Burial:
Hodges Chapel Cemetery
Benson
Johnston County
North Carolina

His name was in a list of minister's names in 1903 in the Free Will Baptist Minutes of Cape Fear Conference, when it met at Hodges Chapel Church, Harnett Co. NC.

Inscription:
Ordained 1898

Raymond Albert Gaskins
Birth:
Jul. 1, 1921
North Carolina
Death:
Nov. 22, 2010
Ayden, Pitt County
North Carolina
Burial:
Ayden Cemetery,
Ayden, Pitt County,
North Carolina

He graduated as salutatorian of his 1938 Ayden High School class, lettering in football and boxing. In 1943 he completed a three-year Coppersmith apprenticeship from the Norfolk Navy Yard and entered the U.S. Navy, serving as a quartermaster in World War II. He returned to Ayden after the war, attending Banking School at UNC-Chapel Hill, while employed with Planter's Bank and Trust Co. Raymond became a minister in 1957, after completing studies at The Free Will Baptist Bible College in Nashville, Tenn. He served as pastor of Liberty Free Will Baptist Church in Ayden from 1958-2004. He met Beatrice Loftin Gaskins in 1946, marrying her in 1947. She preceded him in death after 57 years of marriage.

Rev Earl Hollis Glenn
Birth:
Jan. 6, 1925
Durham
Durham County
North Carolina
Death:
Sep. 24, 2013
Wayne County
North Carolina
Burial:
Wayne Memorial Park
Goldsboro
Wayne County
North Carolina

The Rev. Earl Hollis Glenn, 88, Kitty Askins Hospice Center.
Funeral services at Stoney Creek Original Free Will Baptist Church. The Rev. Johnny Sullivan and the Rev. Barry Williamson officiated. Rev. Glenn was a native of Durham, N.C., the son of Edward D. Glenn and Coy Inez Glenn.

Louis H Green
Birth:
Sep. 26, 1940
Death:
Feb. 18, 1986
Burial:
Sweet Hope Freewill Baptist Church Cemetery,
Pitt County, North Carolina

Jesse Christopher Griffin, Sr
Birth:
June 22, 1879
Nash County,
North Carolina
Death:
1968
North Carolina
Burial:
Cedar Grove Cemetery,
New Bern,
Craven County,
North Carolina

Well-known Free Will Baptist minister, pastor, writer and denominational leader. He was the author of an early Free Will Baptist

Minister's Handbook. He was ordained to the ministry on June 10, 1910 just before his thirty-first birthday.

He attended Eureka College and the Free Will Baptist Seminary at Ayden, North Carolina from 1912 until 1914.

During his 57 years of ministry he pastored 28 churches, conducting numerous revivals, funerals, performing marriage rites, and won scores of people to Christ in a ministry that led from the eastern seashore to the mountains of North Carolina as well as extensive work in many other states.

He united with the Free Will Baptist denomination at the White Oak Hill church in Nash County in 1905.

He was manager of the Free Will Baptist Press 1914-16. His column "Notes and Quotes" appeared in the *Free Will Baptist* for 25 years. He was moderator of the Eastern conference of North Carolina Free Will Baptists 1919-1923. He was a member and served as secretary to the Free Will Baptist Orphanage Board between 1923-28..

He was Vice President of the North Carolina State Association 1931-36. President of the North Carolina State Association 1940-42. Field Sec. North Carolina State Association 1942-45. Publicity Director of the General Conference 1929. Statistician of the General Conference-Eastern General 1933-35.

Chairman of the Treatises Committee of the National Association 1935. Member of the Revision Committee of the Treatise 1940.

Chairman of the Board Of Publications and Literature 1942. Re-elected for five years in 1943. He was a member of the General Board of the National Association and a member of the Executive Committee. He did evangelistic meetings in South Carolina, and Florida, Alabama, Mississippi, Texas, Tennessee and North Carolina. He was the author of many booklets and a book entitled, *The One Foundation*. He was married twice and had a total of 15 children.

Rev Willy Arthur Hales
Birth:
Oct. 29, 1902
North Carolina
Death:
Aug. 12, 1980
North Carolina
Burial:
Maplewood Cemetery
Wilson
Wilson County
North Carolina

He was a Free Will Baptist minister; he was mar. to Ola Taylor (Forbes) Hales. Was an active minister, member of the Eastern General Association of FWB in the 1930's. His name was registered as a minister in its sessions.

Rev Milford H. Hales
Birth:
1898
North Carolina
Death:
1976
North Carolina
Burial:
Mount Zion FWB Church
Cemetery
Wilson County, North Carolina

Rev James J. Hall
Birth:
Nov. 3, 1849
England
Death:
Jul. 9, 1921
Harlem
Columbia County
Georgia
Burial:
Cross Creek Cemetery #3
Fayetteville
Cumberland County
North Carolina
Burial:
Cross Creek Cemetery #3
Fayetteville
Cumberland County
North Carolina

An ordained minister in the 1935
Minutes of the Old Western
Conference of the Free Will Baptist

Rev. J. J. Hall, son of S.E. and Eliza
(Combs) Hall, was born in London,
Eng. He was educated at
Spurgeon's College, London, and in
1870 married Angelina Bartlett.
Coming to this country, he was
ordained July 9, 1871, and became
pastor of the churches at East
Farnham, Quebec, and Enosburgh
Falls, VT, serving them three years.
After a pastorate of two years
(1874-76) at Waterloo, IA, he was

pastor of the Pine Street church, Manchester, NH, 1879-80; at Auburn, ME, 1880-86; and at Minneapolis, Minn, 1886-88.

Additions to these churches were received during these years. Brother Hall aided in establishing the Ocean Park Association, Maine, was secretary and treasurer of the Maine Central Yearly Meeting, was six years on the Maine Home Mission Board, and for a time president of the Western Association.

Rev James J. Hall
BIRTH
3 Nov 1849
England
DEATH
9 Jul 1921 (aged 71)
Harlem, Columbia County, Georgia, USA
BURIAL
Cross Creek Cemetery #3
Fayetteville, Cumberland County, North Carolina, USA

"Rev. J. J. Hall, son of S.E. and Eliza (Combs) Hall, was born in London, Eng.. He was educated at Spurgeon's College, London, and in 1870 married Angelina Bartlett. Coming to this country, he was ordained July 9, 1871, and became pastor of the churches at East Farnham, Quebec, and Enosburgh Falls, VT, serving them three years. After a pastorate of two years (1874-76) at Waterloo, IA, he was pastor of the Pine Street church, Manchester, NH, 1879-80; at Auburn, ME, 1880-86; and at Minneapolis, Minn., 1886-88. Additions to these churches were received during these years. Brother Hall aided in establishing the Ocean Park Association, Maine, was secretary and treasurer of the Maine Central Yearly Meeting (YM), was six years on the Maine Home Mission Board, and for a time president of the Western Association."--from "Cyclopedia of Free Baptists," pub. 1889, by Burgess and Ward.

John Hall, Jr
Birth:
Unknown
Death:
Mar. 11, 1992
Reidsville, Rockingham County, North Carolina
Burial:
Evergreen Memory Gardens, Reidsville, Rockingham County, North Carolina

He organized a Free Will Baptist Church in Readsville in 1977 as a home mission's project. He served as moderator of the Maryland State Association and editor of the Maryland Newsletter. He had been a schoolteacher, principal and administrator. He attended Free Will Baptist Bible College, Maryland Bible Institute, Covington Theological Seminary and Elkton Bible College.

David Wells Hansley
Birth:
Dec. 21, 1909
Folkstone,
Onslow Co. N.C.
Death:
Apr. 24, 1989
Burial:
Dalys Chapel
Free Will Baptist Church

Cemetery,
Liddell
Lenoir County, North Carolina

He was an active leader as Chairman of the Board of Directors that led in the creation of the Mount Olive College in North Carolina, a role he held from 1953 to 1963, but continued on the board until 1970. He was a member of the Board of Directors for the Free Will Baptist Press, Ayden, N.C., Chairman of Board of Superannuation and League Board of the National Association. He was a grandson of Jesse Heath an early FWB preacher. He became a minister in 1930 at the age of 21 and served 37 churches in 15 N.C. counties from 1931-1988.

Rev Wingate Aquilla Hansley
BIRTH
30 Dec 1928
Durham, Durham County,
North Carolina
DEATH
24 Jul 1997 (aged 68)
Jacksonville, Onslow County,

North Carolina, USA
BURIAL
Kirby Family Cemetery
Kenly, Johnston County,
North Carolina

Rev Charlie Jackson Harris, Sr
Birth:
1870
North Carolina, USA
Death:
1943
Pitt County
North Carolina
Burial:
Greenwood Cemetery
Greenville
Pitt County, North Carolina

He was the first Field Secretary for the North Carolina State Convention when it was organized in 1913.

Rev William Harris
Birth:
May, 1810
Death:
Nov. 30, 1893
Burial:
Pleasant Grove Free Will Baptist
Church Cemetery
Dunn
Harnett County, North Carolina
Eld. Wm. Harris' ministry dates back to the infancy of the Cape Fear Conference [ed. abt 1850]. Eld. Harris was a man of very much energy in the calling wherewith he was called. In the beginning of his ministerial labors he was a very successful ingatherer to the conference...His manner of preaching was very plain and stately. Though uneducated, his familiarity with the word of God was hardly excelled. Like many others, he was actuainted with sorrow, tribulations and disappoint-ments. We believe that his last days were his happiest ones.He attended the annual conference held with the church at Shady Grove, in Sampson county, 1893. He went home from the conference and immediately he was taken sick with pneumonia and died in the latter part of the year, 1893. "Blessed are the dead which die in the Lord."--from Minutes of Cape Fear Conference

Inscription:
He died as he lived trusting in God

Bobby E. Harrell
Birth:
Jul. 1, 1933
Death:
Unknown
Burial:
Dalys Chapel Free Will
Baptist Church Cemetery,
Liddell,
Lenoir County,
North Carolina

Thaddeus F. Harrison
Birth:
March 8, 1878
Washington County
North Carolina
Death:
October 24, 1897
Ayden, Pitt County,
North Carolina
Burial:
Ayden Cemetery,
Ayden, Pitt County,
North Carolina

His family gave him all the advantages of an education that they possibly could in his early life.. In 1884 he went to Plymouth High School, then to the Academy at Pantego to study under Prof. A. L. Johnson for 10 months. From there he went to the Carolina Institute to study under Prof. Rightsell. And from there to Chapel Hill after which he returned home and taught school. Sometime before his last schooling he united with the Disciples church. Not long after he commenced exhorting and speaking in public and soon became dissatisfied and united with the Free Will Baptist at Union Chapel in January of 1894 and was ordained in the same year. He and his twin brother (Theodore) published two books and pamphlets, one containing 10 sermons and the other was on feet washing.. Later he wrote two more pamphlets, one was 100 facts on baptism and another on feet washing. In the spring of 1896 Elder Harrison decided to write a history of the Free Will Baptist of North Carolina. Thus he became a co-author of the *History of North Carolina Free Will Baptist* with J.M. Barfield.

Edward David Hathaway, Sr
Birth:
Jul. 28, 1849
Belvoir
Pitt County,
North Carolina,
Death:
Feb. 2, 1919

Greenville
Pitt County, North Carolina
Burial:
Hathaway Family Cemetery
Belvoir
Pitt County,
North Carolina

was a pastor of Gum Swamp and other churches, but remained a member of Gum Swamp until his death.

He wrote about the early movement and was an editor of the first paper in North Carolinia. He is remembered here. Son of Howell Hearn & Sarah Elmina Randolph.

Elder Rufus K. Hearn
Birth:
Oct. 20, 1819
Pitt County,North Carolina
Death:
Mar. 3, 1894
Pitt County
North Carolina
Burial:
Gum Swamp Freewill Baptist
Church Cemetery
Greenville
Pitt County
North Carolina

He was a leading minister in the mid-1800 until his death in the NC Free Will Baptist movement. Also,

Jeremiah Heath
Birth:
Oct. 4, 1793
North Carolin
Death:
Feb. 22, 1867
Cove City
Craven County, North Carolina
Burial:
Heath Family Cemetery
Craven County, North Carolina

An early Free Will Baptist minister in a remnant of churches in 1832 from the Philadelphia Association. Rev. Jeremiah HEATH's name is found among historical records with early FWB minister's names who contended for, and remained influential in sustaining the Orig. Free Will Baptist church in its early formation and growth, especially the old Bethel Conference, when it could have been merged. He was a leader, with others, during this time who carried forward the FWB cause. Jeremiah was a prominent surveyor in the early formation of the area, to which land records attest; also, he was a Free Will Baptist minister. He organized the Core Creek FWB Church, and also pastored the FWB church at New Bern, NC, and probably others. He raised several children who became worthy citizens. Rev. Jesse Heath's name is known as a prominent leader in the area. (Family papers are held in Joyner Library, East Carolina University, Greenville, N.C. --Index is online). Parents: Rigdon and Elizabeth (Jackson) HEATH. Spouse: Clemmie Holland Jones (NC mar rec'ds)

Inscription:
Organized Core Creek Free Will Baptist Church 1865.

John David Hill
Birth:
Sep. 30, 1924
North Carolina
Death:
Nov. 10, 2008
North Carolina
Burial:
Bethel Original
Freewill Baptist Church Cemetery,
Four Oaks, Johnston County,
North Carolina

Milton Aaron Hollifield, Sr
Birth:
Apr. 19, 1926
Mitchell County, North Carolina
Death:
Jul. 14, 2014
Swannanoa
Buncombe County, North Carolina
Burial:
Old Fort City Cemetery
Old Fort
McDowell County, North Carolina

He was the son of the late George and Annie Baucombe Hollifield. For over 60 years, Rev. Hollifield was a caring and dedicated Free Will Baptist Minister having served in McDowell, Haywood and Buncombe Counties and in Wayne, MI. and was active in the work of several committees and boards of the National Association of the Free Will Baptist. Pastor Hollifield organized and was a promotional representative for the Free Will Baptist Blue Ridge Association in Western North Carolina. He was a member and care pastor of Rocky Pass Free Will Baptist Church in Marion. He fulfilled his passion for evangelism through his involvement in conducting revivals in numerous states and other countries.

Rev. Hollifield was passionate about visiting hospitals, nursing homes and the homebound. He was a charter member of the board of Directors of the Swannanoa Valley Medical Center. An autobiography was published about his life entitled "Why Me Lord".Revs. Milton Hollifield, Jr., Steve Lytle and Alan Sailors officiated.

G W Homes
Birth:
Unknown
Death:
Unknown
Burial:
Maple Springs Baptist Church
Cemetery
Louisburg
Franklin County
North Carolina
Plot: Plot # 37

Rev. G. W. Homes' name is in list of ordained Free Will Baptist ministers, in the Western Conference minutes, when in 49th Session convened in 1935.

Elder Curtis Daniel Howell, Sr
Birth:
Jan. 4, 1836
Goldsboro
Wayne County
North Carolina
Death:
Apr. 9, 1921
Wayne County
North Carolina
Burial:
Deans Cemetery
Goldsboro
Wayne County
North Carolina

Father: Morris Howell. Mother: Mary Polly Deans Howell
Eld. Curtis D. Howell, was a native of NC, born near, and dying near Goldsboro.
He served in the Civil War until its close in 1865. He professed religion soon after returning home and joined the M.E. Church. About 1894, he withdrew and joined the Free Will Baptist at Stony Hill Church in Wayne County.

He was faithful to his charge as a minister. It seemed his mission was to build up weak churches.

He was twice married: first, to Miss Sophia Deans, Feb. 6, 1868; to this union.

In Sept. 1912, he was married to Miss Josephine West, who died a few days after

Elder Howell. An ordained Free Will Baptist minister/leader in the Western Conference in NC

He was a good man, and has gone to his final reward."--taken from 1921 Minutes of the 35th Session of the Western Conference, when convened at Holly Springs Church, Johnston Co. NC.

Elder Curtis Daniel Howell, Sr
BIRTH   4 Jan 1836
Goldsboro, Wayne County, North Carolina, USA
DEATH   9 Apr 1921 (aged 85)
Wayne County, North Carolina, USA
BURIAL
Deans Cemetery
Goldsboro, Wayne County, North Carolina, USA

Eld. Curtis D. Howell, was a native of NC, born near, and dying near Goldsboro.

He served in the Civil War unti its close in 1865. He professed religion soon after returning home and joined the M.E. Church. About 1894, he withdrew and joined the Free Will Baptist at Stony Hill Church in Wayne County.

He was faithful to his charge as a minister. It seemed his mission was to build up weak churches.

He was twice married: first, to Miss Sophia Deans, Feb. 6, 1868; to this union was born four boys and one daughter. Three survive him.

In Sept. 1912, he was married to Miss Josephine West, who died a few days after Elder Howell.

He was a good man and has gone to his final reward."

--taken from 1921 Minutes of the 35th Session of the Western Conference, when

convened at Holly Springs Church, Johnston Co. NC.An ordained Free Will Baptist minister/leader in the Western Conference in NC. He was also a veteran of the Civil War, serving until its close.

Elder W. M. Howell
Birth:
Dec. 1, 1866
Death:
Aug. 13, 1929
Burial:
Pike Cemetery
Pikeville
Wayne County
North Carolina

Rev. W. M. Howell, was the son of Robert B. Howell, and Zilphia Howell. He married Ora Pannell Dec. 9, 1914, Wayne Co. NC.

He was an ordained Free Will Baptist minister/pastor in the Western Conference of Original FWB churches, which included Wayne County. His name appears in leadership positions in old Conference Minutes (1916) as being moderator of the Conference, and again re-elected the next session. Unknown are the churches he pastored and other fields of labor in which he worked. He was a leader and an asset to his church and the area in which he ministered.

Danny H Howell
Birth:
Oct. 19, 1946
Death:
Sep. 4, 1993
Burial:
Fairview Cemetery
La Grange
Lenoir County, North Carolina

While working in the church gymnasium, he climbed a ladder and had a fall which caused his death at age 46. He was called to preach in 1977 and was ordained to the ministry in 1981 pastoring two North Carolina churches; Morehead City and the Goshen church in Mt. Holly. He attended Free Will Baptist Bible College and Lenore Community College, North Carolina and received his Doctor of Ministries from Bethany Theological Seminary, Dothan, Alabama.

Clint Hardrick Holt
Birth:
Mar. 31, 1915
North Carolina
Death:
Dec. 19, 2009
Johnston County, North Carolina
Burial:
Selma Memorial Gardens, Selma, Johnston County, North Carolina

Holt retired from the NC Dept. of Transportation and was a Free Will Baptist Minister for most of his adult life. He lived in Hendersonville before moving to Smithfield in the early 1980's.

Rev Eugene A. W. Husketh
Birth:
Aug. 7, 1857
Death:
May 1, 1931
Burial:
Lewis Augustus Wilson Cemetery
New Light
Wake County, North Carolina

An ordained Free Will Baptist minister whose name was shown in a minister's list of church conference minutes in 1920. Parents shown as William Husketh & Maria Wilson (both b Granville Co.

Onslow Memorial Park, Jacksonville, Onslow County, North Carolina

Billy was the pastor of the Cardinal Village Free Will Baptist Church that grew from 30 to a total of 350. He had a high Sunday of 525 on Easter one year. He was truly a man who cared for the people of his church and the entire community. His church loved him so much that they paid for his resting place and for the headstones for he and his wife. His son, Kevin, follows his father in the ministry.

Billy Gray Jackson
Birth:
Jul. 27, 1934
Wilson, Wilson County,
North Carolina
Death:
Mar. 2, 1997
Chapel Hill,
Madison County, North Carolina
Burial:

Robert Copps Jackson
Birth:
November 19, 1865
Sampson County,
North Carolina,
Death:
June 21, 1908
North Carolina
Burial:
Roberts Grove

Free Will Baptist Church,
Dunn
Sampson County,
North Carolina

As a young man he joined a Missionary Baptist Church where he was a very faithful member, but in July of 1887 he severed his relationship with this church and united with the Free Will Baptist Church at Shady Grove where he held his membership for several years until he organized a new Free Will Baptist Church near his home. He was licensed to the ministry on August 1, 1891 and the next year in 1892 he was ordained to the ministry. He served for 17 years as a preacher of the gospel of Christ his ministry took him beyond his own state into South Carolina and even as far north as Ohio in his evangelistic work. He was active in the Cape Fear Conference, establishing several Churches of the Free Will Baptist faith.

Roy H Jackson
Birth:
Jun. 20, 1901
Death:
Aug. 31, 1991
Burial:

Pleasant Grove Free Will Baptist
Church Cemetery,
Dunn, Harnett County,
North Carolina

Rev Hannibal Washington Jernigan, Sr
Birth:
Sep. 11, 1849
Mingo
Sampson County, North Carolina
Death:
Jan. 22, 1942
Dunn
Harnett County, North Carolina
Burial:
Stoney Run Pentecostal FWB Church
Sampson County, North Carolina

In a list of ministers in Minutes of 1903 Cape Fear Conference, which met at Hodges Chapel Church, Harnett Co. NC.

Rev Isaac W Jernigan
Birth:
Dec. 15, 1898
Death:
Aug. 31, 1968
Burial:
Spring Hope Memorial Gardens
Spring Hope

Nash Count, North Carolina

A Free Will Baptist minister, who ministered in Bailey, and other churches in Nash Co. and was pastor at rose Bud, Wilson, in 1935-36.

Walter L. Jernigan
Birth:
Mar. 21, 1900
Bladen County, North Carolina
Death:
Nov. 19, 1962
Bladenboro,
Bladen County, North Carolina
Burial:
Lewis Cemetery, Bladenboro,
Bladen County, North Carolina

An ordained Free Will Baptist minister and pastor.

Milton Lee Johnson
Birth:
Aug. 19, 1915
Johnston Co., North Carolina
Death:
February 11 1969
Middlesex

Nash Co., North Carolina
Burial:
Marsh Swamp Church Cemetery,
Wilson, North Carolina

He was a well-known pastor and did a remarkable work throughout the denomination. He was Business Manager of Mount Olive Junior College between 1956-61 He served as the Superintendent of the Free Will Baptist orphanage in Middlesex a total of six years before a heart attack took his life.

Rev Calvin B Jones
Birth:
Sep. 1, 1873
Augusta
Richmond County
Georgia
Death:
Dec. 19, 1957
Winston-Salem
Forsyth County
North Carolina
Burial:
Evergreen Cemetery
Winston-Salem
Forsyth County
North Carolina

Name in a roll of ministers from Old Central Conference and its districts.

Rev James Read Jones
Birth:
Nov. 29, 1840
Death:
Jul. 21, 1925
Burial:
New Garden Friends Cemetery
Greensboro
Guilford County
North Carolina

Rev. J.R. Jones, of Cape Fear Conference was present at the 1916 Western Conf. which met in Johnston Co. NC, Oct. 1916.

Daniel Andrew Jordan, Jr
Birth:
Dec. 7, 1924
Death:
Jan. 26, 2016
Burial:
Evergreen Memorial Park
Wilson
Wilson County
North Carolina

Daniel Andrew Jordan, Jr., 91, of Mooresville passed away and The

Rev. Rudy Owens will officiated.

Alan Clinton Joyner
Birth:
Oct. 8, 1963
Wilson County, North Carolina
Death:
Oct. 24, 2011
Burial:
Queen Anne Cemetery
Fountain
Pitt County, North Carolina

Son of Llewellyn Brann Joyner and the late Clinton Hubert Joyner, he was a graduate of Wilson Christian Academy. He attended Atlantic Christian College (Barton College) and graduated from Mount Olive College in 2005. He was ordained as an minister in the Original Free Baptist denomination. He served as pastor of the Free Union OFWB Church for eight years where his funeral was held on October 28, 2011, with The Rev. Kelley Smith and The Rev. Dr. David Hines officiating.

Rev George Joyner
Birth:
Oct. 16, 1823
Pitt County, North Carolina
Death:
Sep. 12, 1885
Kinston
Lenoir County, North Carolina
Burial:
Hollywood Cemetery, Farmville
Pitt County, North Carolina
Reverend George Joyner was the son of J. and C. Joyner and husband of Louisa A. Blount Joyner. Rev. George Joyner, a native of this county, died at his home in Kinston on last Thursday. His remains were brought to Marlboro on Friday for interment. He was a most excellent and devout man and his death is much regretted.

Rev Grover Cleveland Joyner
Birth:
1893
Death:
1966
Burial:
Sunset Memorial Park
Smithfield
Johnston County, North Carolina

An ordained Free Will Baptist minister.

On That Bright And Cloudless Morning When The Dead In Christ Shall Rise

Charles Edward Keith
Birth:
Jun. 15, 1922
Dickenson County, Virginia
Death:
Mar. 9, 2008,
Sanford,
Lee County, North Carolina
Burial:
Markham Memorial Gardens,
Durham,
Durham County, North Carolina

A Free Will Baptist minister serving churches in North and South Carolina. Father of N.C. Promotional Director Billy Keith.

Eld. Robert C. Kennedy
Birth:
1881
Death:
1954
Burial:
Whaley Cemetery,
Duplin, County, North Carolina
His son was Rev. Rashie Kennedy (1911 - 2012) who lived to be 100

years of age. He was in the first graduating class of Free Will Baptist Bible College, Nashville, Tennessee in 1942. His ministry among Free Will Baptists is well recorded not only here but in heaven.

Rashie Kennedy, Sr
Birth:
Jul. 15, 1911
Duplin County, North Carolina
Death:
Jun. 19, 2012
Beulaville, Duplin County,
North Carolina
Burial:
East Duplin Memorial Gardens,
Beulaville, Duplin County,
North Carolina

Converted at age 11, Kennedy was licensed to preach in 1940 and ordained in 1941. His 70-year ministry was marked by a passion for prayer and evangelism. Reverend Kennedy sold his North Carolina home in 1942 and relocated to Nashville, Tn., with his wife and two children to attend FWBBC. He was 31 at the time, three years older than the college president, Dr. L.C. Johnson. While a student at FWBBC, Kennedy organized and pastored Sylvan Park Free Will Baptist Church in West Nashville. He graduated in 1945 and later pastored in North Carolina, Texas, Florida, and Louisiana. His denominational service included eight years on the Free Will Baptist International Missions Board, six years on the Home Missions Board, two years as Texas Executive Secretary, two years on the Oklahoma Bible College (now Hillsdale FWB College) Board and other district and state boards in North Carolina and Texas. He and Myrtle Kennedy were married 63 years. He started a writing career at age 90 by embracing Internet technology and creating a website that featured many of his articles and sermons.

Needham Sanders Lancaster

Birth:
May 5, 1884
Wayne County,
North Carolina
Death:
Nov. 16, 1928
Onslow County,
North Carolina
Burial:
Pate Cemetery
Stoney Creek
Wayne County,
North Carolina

Ordained a minister, 4th Sun. Aug. 1915, of the Orig. Free Will Baptist Church.

Rev Austin Graham Lane

BIRTH
20 Aug 1921
North Carolina, USA
DEATH
2 Sep 2016 (aged 95)
Craven County, North Carolina, USA
BURIAL
Pine Tree Cemetery
Ernul, Craven County, North Carolina, USA

Rev. Austin Graham Lane, 95, of Ernul, passed away Friday, September 2, 2016, at home. He served in the U.S. Army, receiving the Purple Heart. He was a farmer and ordained Free Will Baptist Minister for over 65 years. He served numerous churches and held numerous offices in the Free Will Baptist Convention and local conference. He was also an Ethic Coordinator for Home Missions serving the LAO Evangelical Church and Hispanic Community. His funeral at Trent Free Will Baptist Church with the Rev. David Hansley officiating. An ordained Free Will Baptist minister for over 60 years. WW II Army Veteran and recipient of the Purple Heart.

Rev James Merritt Langdon
Birth:
Feb. 10, 1863
Johnston County
North Carolina, USA
Death
Oct. 12, 1910
Johnston County, North Carolina
Burial:
Benson City Cemetery
Benson
Johnston County, North Carolina,

An ordained Freewill Bapt. minister, whose name was in a list of ministers in the 1903 E. Conference, meeting in Harnett Co. NC. "He was ordained in 1900 and preached at the Benson Free Will Baptist Church till his death in 1910.Parents Merritt Langdon and Margaret I Stephenson were married on December 31st 1856.

Rev Jack D. Lassiter
Birth
Unknown
Durham,
Durham County,
North Carolina
Death
25 Mar 2018
Greenville, Pitt County,
North Carolina,
Burial
Evergreen Memorial Park
Wilson, Wilson County,
North Carolina,

Evangelist Jack Lassiter, 62, he was transported from this earth to his heavenly home to be with the Lord he loved and served for 41 years. Mr. Lassiter is survived by his wife of 37 years, Alane Vester Lassiter, originally from Wilson; and his brother, Tim Lassiter, of Durham. He was preceded in death by his parents, Jackie and Laura Lassiter, who were lifelong residents of Durham.

He is a graduate of Southern High School in Durham and Atlantic Christian College in Wilson. He was awarded an honorary Doctor of Divinity by Emmaus Bible College in Elizabethton and a Doctorate of Letters by Bethany Christian College in Alabama. During his ministry he served as pastor of several Free Will Baptist churches, director of Public Relations and Fund Raising at Southeastern FWB College at Wendell. His final years in ministry were spent as a traveling evangelist in numerous states across the country. While in evangelism, the Rev. Lassiter recorded five projects of gospel songs and hymns as well as numerous sermon projects. Evangelist Lassiter became disabled and had been confined to his home since 2012.

Rev Lunda Lee
Birth:
Jun. 24, 1854
Death:
Oct. 20, 1917
Burial:
Lee Cemetery
Sampson County, North Carolina

His name is in a list of ordained ministers in Minutes of 1903 Cape Fear Conference, which met at Hodges Chapel Church, Harnett Co. NC.

John W Lucas
Birth:
Oct. 23, 1857
Death:
Jun. 14, 1925
Burial:
Pleasant Grove Free Will Baptist Church Cemetery
Dunn,
Harnett County North Carolina

Reverend J. W. Lucas, a graduate of Wake Forest, was born Averysboro, N. C. in 1850, and was ordained in 1872. For over a quarter of a century, he served as a Free Will Baptist minister and as an educator in East Tennessee. Most of this time he was affiliated with the Union Association. He served as principal of high schools at Parrotsville, Midway, and elsewhere. He succeeded Brother Woolsey as pastor of the Woolsey College Church. His work at the college both as teacher and as pastor was outstanding in quality.

He was in attendance at the General Conference at Harper's Ferry, West Virginia, 1901 and again along with Dr. T. H. Woolsey at Hillsdale, Michigan in 1904.-- from One Hundred Years of Paul Woolsey's Free Will Baptist Family, pub. 1949.

An early Free Will Baptist minister.

Patrick Thomas "Elder" Lucas
Birth:
Sep. 8, 1854
North Carolina
Death:
Jul. 2, 1912
Wilson County, North Carolina
Burial:
Lucas Cemetery, Lucama,
Wilson County, North Carolina

Malachi Daniel Lucas
Birth:
Mar. 12, 1884
Wilson County, North Carolina
Death:
Jun. 14, 1909
Wilson County, North Carolina
Burial:
Lucas Cemetery,
Lucama,Wilson County,
North Carolina

Alice Voliva Lupton
Birth:
Oct. 13, 1875
Death:
Jan. 24, 1962
Burial:
Cedar Grove Cemetery,
New Bern, Craven County,
North Carolina

She was one of the earliest organizers for women within the denomination. She organized the first "lady's aid society" in the St. Mary's church in the historic city of New Bern. In May of 1927, a state women's convention was organized in Goldsboro, North Carolina where Mrs. Lupton became the first president of the statewide organization. The 1928 session met at the Eureka College at Ayden, where the work was departmentalized with directors for missions, Christian education, Superannuation, stewardship and youth training. In 1935, a national auxiliary convention was organized at Black Jack church, near Greenville. The North Carolina convention affiliated with it and Mrs. Lupton became it's first president and the North Carolina women joined with others in working toward a Bible college and a foreign missions program. From the earliest days of the women's movement Alice Lupton was always seen at the forefront. She was a author and columnist writing for the *Free Will Baptists* for many years a woman's column. She freely wrote programs for the women's movement and also was the author of one book, *Footprints Of Jesus* which was widely used by women's auxiliaries and ministers and in pre-Easter observations.

William Howard Lupton, Sr
Birth:
Mar. 5, 1851
Lowland
Pamlico County, North Carolina
Death:
Aug. 19, 1888
Lowland
Pamlico County, North Carolina
Burial:
Mercer Cemetery
Lowland
Pamlico County, North Carolina

Spouse: Ellenor Susan Johnson Ireland (1854 - 1938). Children: Charles B. Lupton (1877 - 1953), William Howard Lupton (1878 - 1962) and Alice Lupton Mayo (1889 - 1978).

Note: He was buried in the back of the cemetery near the woods with a wooden marker. Time and weather deteriorated the marker.

Rev Leonard Benjamin Manning
Birth:
May 13, 1900
Pitt County
North Carolina
Death:
Apr. 20, 1985
Greenville

Pitt County
North Carolina
Burial:
Queen Anne Cemetery
Fountain
Pitt County
North Carolina

Rev. L. B. Manning was the son of Joseph Alonzo Manning and Martha "Mattie" Hamilton Manning. In 1951 list of NC ministers in the state association.

Rev Thomas Calvin Marks
Birth:
Jun. 28, 1873
Stanly County
North Carolina
Death:
Jul. 18, 1941
Durham
Durham County
North Carolina
Burial:

Woodlawn Memorial Park
Durham
Durham County
North Carolina

Rev, T.C. Marks, was an ordained Free Will Baptist minister that served churches in the area where he lived. His name was in the Minutes of the 49th Session of the Western Conference of FWB in 1935. Married to Alice Rebecca Lockamy around 1895. Son of James Marks and Mary Rickford Marks.

William Royster Martin
Birth:
Unknown
Death:
Unknown
North Carolina
Burial:
Micro Memorial Gardens
Cemetery
Johnston County
North Carolina

Reverend William Royster Martin Micro-, age 68, pastor of Holly Springs Free Will Baptist Church on Kenly was a retired fertilizer and chemical dealer and a US Navy veteran of WW II. He was a former member and chairman of the Johnston County Board of Education. He was a member of Kenly Masonic Lodge # 257, a member of the Scottish rite, and was a Shriner. Rev. Martin was also a member of the Western Conference Board of Ordination of Original Free Will Baptist Churches

and a member of Micro Free Will Baptist Church.
The Rev. Clyde Cox and Rev. Dewey Boling will officiated

Thomas Hillman Matthews
Birth:
Oct. 9, 1830
Nash County,
North Carolina
Death:
Sep. 7, 1918
Nash County, North Carolina
Burial:
Thomas H. Matthews Cemetery,
Nash County,
North Carolina

Thomas was a Free Will Baptist Minister and served in the Civil War as a Private in the Civil War during 1861-1865, Confederate Regiment State Origin: North Carolina he married Martha Bass on December 2, 1852 in Nash County, North Carolina.

Rev Robert McNabb
BIRTH
19 Feb 1805
DEATH
17 Oct 1851 (aged 46)
BURIAL
Carthage United Methodist Church Cemetery
Carthage, Moore County, North Carolina, USA

He was married to Elizabeth McAlister Thames McNabb whose dates are 1811–1883. An active minister in the Free Will Baptist Church, who is mentioned in church history, in N.Carolina in the early years. He wrote a letter to NH to church paper, Morning Star, in 1828.

Rev Harry Edward Mintz
Birth: Sep. 7, 1932
North Carolina,
Death: Oct. 6, 2017
Loudon
Loudon County
Tennessee,
Burial:
Garrett-Hillcrest Memorial Park
Waynesville
Haywood County
North Carolina,

He preached and pastored for sixty years at various churches. Preceded in death by wife, Edith Mintz; parents, Robert and Mae Mintz; and several brothers and sisters. Survived by children: Imogene Nix and husband, Earl of Loudon, Lynn Harris and husband, Jerry of Erwin, and Harry Mintz, Jr. and wife, Lisa of Myrtle Beach; grandchildren, Amy (Tim) Curtis, Brandy (Larry) Robinson, Andrea (Mark) Albright, Ben Mintz, and Sam Mintz; and great grandchildren, Emma and Aly Curtis, Landon, Elijah and Levi Albright, Bailey, Macy, Ezekiel and Josiah Robinson. Rev. Larry Robinson will be officiating.

William Moses Monk
Birth:
Jul. 1, 1877
Sampson County, North Carolina
Death:
Oct. 30, 1959
Bell Arthur,
Pitt County, North Carolina
Burial:
Arthur Chapel
FWB Church Cemetery,
Bell Arthur, Pitt County,
North Carolina

Monk was the founding pastor of Arthur Chapel Free Will Baptist Church.

Alfred Moore
Birth:
May 28, 1813
Death:
Aug. 28, 1870
Lenoir County, North Carolina

Burial:
Moore Family Cemetery
Hugo, Lenoir County,
North Carolina

Rev. Alfred Moore was a Free Will Baptist minister for 38 years. He was 59 yrs when he died, leaving his widow and children to mourn his passing. His ministerial work was with the remnant of his church which labored to spread the word after severe hardships. He remained with the part of the dissenting Free Will Baptists who declined to merge with a Disciples coalition in about 1832. His name appears in other records and books. The churches he pastored, are not known, but he remained a faithful minister until death. Several of his children are buried in this cemetery.

Elder J. W. Moore
Birth:
Sep. 22, 1845
North Carolina
Death:
Jan. 27, 1932
North Carolina
Burial:
Bethel Original Freewill Baptist
Church Cemetery,
Four Oaks,
Johnston County,,
North Carolina

Parents: Henry Moore (1821 - 1884) - Culia Ann Beasley Moore (1832 - 1917)
Spouse: Mary E Lee Moore (1860 - 1923)*
Children: George Edward Moore (1869 - 1931)- Norsissa Moore Faircloth (1872 - 1928)-Ida Moore McLamb (1874 - 1947)- John Ira Moore (1876 - 1962)- James Henry Moore (1878 - 1944)- Lonnie D Moore (1881 - 1954)-Jesse B Moore (1882 - 1959)- Willie Allen Moore (1893 - 1964)-Joseph Randle Moore (1894 - 1969)- Dora Mae Moore Blackman (1896 - 1959)- Allie Hawkins Moore Martin (1900 - 1984).
Siblings:
John Wesley Moore (1845 - 1932)
James H Moore (1845 - 1931)
Britta Ann Moore Stanley (1848 - 1920).

J. H. Moore
Birth:
Sep. 11, 1874
Death:

Nov. 6, 1950
Burial:
Sweet Hope Freewill Baptist
Church Cemetery,
Pitt County, North Carolina

James Moore
Birth:
March 20, 1793
Edgecombe Co.
North Carolina
Death:
1882
Greene County,
North Carolina
Burial:
Free Union Church Cemetery,
Greene County,
North Carolina

He moved from Edgecombe County to Greene County at a very young age and joined the Grimsley Free Will Baptist Church. He accepted the call to preach and was licensed in January 1825 and ordained in February 1827.
He became a very active preacher taking care of many churches in the area. In 1850 he started a church in

Greene County that will he named Free Union. It became a flourishing church and he remained a member of the church until his departure in July 1882. Elder Moore served for 53 years as a faithful Minister. Elder J.M. Barfield heard him preach his last sermon which was a funeral service. He was so feeble that two man sat behind him ready to catch him should he began to fall. He had to be ushered in and out of the church building. His funeral was preached by brother Barfield who used the 13th and 14th chapters of the book of Revelation.

John Moore
Birth:
Jun. 1, 1832
Death:
Dec. 13, 1889
Burial:
Hodges Chapel Free Will Baptist
Cemetery,
Harnett County, North Carolina

Eld. John Moore was a native of Harnett County, N. C., where he was converted and began to hold prayer-meetings, and was ordained to preach the Gospel, Oct. 13. 1874. He served the remainder of his life in the Master's cause and to Christianize this part of God's moral vineyard.

Elder John Wesley Moore
BIRTH
22 Sep 1845
Johnston County, North Carolina,
USA
DEATH   27 Jan 1932 (aged 86)
Johnston County, North Carolina,
USA
BURIAL
Bethel Original Freewill Baptist
Church Cemetery
Four Oaks, Johnston County,
North Carolina, USA

An early Free Will Baptist minister who first married Elizabeth Hawkins Lee on 25 Feb 1869; After she passed, he married Mary Elizabeth Lee on 24 May 1891

Rev Thomas Moore
Birth:
Dec. 22, 1826
Death:
Aug. 13, 1898
Burial:
Elaney Woods Cemetery
Snow Hill
Greene County
North Carolina

There is old Minutes of the NC Orig. Free Will Baptist Gen. Conf., held at Kit Swamp Meeting House, Craven Co. NC, in 1854, with a list of ministers, and one is Rev. Thomas Moore.

Edward C Morris
Birth:
Aug. 16, 1891
Death:
Oct. 21, 1976
Burial:
Woodlawn Memorial Park,
Durham,
Durham County, North Carolina,
Plot: Section 5,
Lock 12, Lot 15

He moved to Georgia from North Carolina in 1942 to pastor the Glennville and Ebenezer churches in Glennville which at the time were half-time churches. He was the first full-time promotional director in the state of Georgia beginning in 1947 serving through 1961. He worked to unite the state of Georgia. He started printing and sending out a monthly paper which was named *Promotional Bulletin* which is still in use today by the state of Georgia. He was known as a leader, promotional director, editor and publisher, and had an interested in the state youth camp program. During his time the work in Georgia grew and even land given to the state in 1948 for the youth camp. Many new churches were formed, joining the state association which had begun in 1937. By 1953 the state of Georgia had 127 churches. Even though the state Association was relatively young at the time. The Chattahoochee Association was the oldest Association being organized in 1842 and was the first to have all of its churches participating in the state work. After his resignation in 1961 Rev. Morris returned to North Carolina.

J R Morris, Jr
Birth:
Feb. 15, 1881
North Carolina
Death:
Oct. 24, 1921
North Carolina
Burial:
Branch Chapel Free Will Baptist
Church
Smithfield
Johnston County
,North Carolina

A minister in the Original Free will Baptist Western Conference.

James Clayton Moye
Birth:
Jul. 19, 1890
Greene County, North Carolina
Death:
May 21, 1961
Wilson, North Carolina
Burial:
Snow Hill Cemetery,
Snow Hill,
Greene County,
North Carolina

He attended Ayden Seminary and the Whitsett Institute afterwards, serving Free Will Baptist churches as pastor in. Pitt, Green and Lenoir counties, but had to retire in 1949 because of failing health. He served in the North Carolina General Assembly as the Representative from Greene County for three terms, 1929, 1931 and 1933. He was Mayor of Snow Hill for six years and served on the Snow Hill School Board. He was also on the Board of Directors of the Free Will Baptist Children's Home in Middlesex. He was a former moderator of the North Carolina Free Will Baptist Convention and was a benefactor of the Free Will Baptist College in Mt. Olive. J. C. Moye Library was named in his honor. He was an extensive farmer and also operated a Chevrolet dealership in the Snow Hill for 27 years.

Richard Evans McKeel
Birth:
Jan. 31, 1948
Death:
Dec. 21, 2015
Burial:
Evans Cemetery
Pine Level
Johnston County
North Carolina

Rev. Richard E. McKeel, 67, of Selma, went home to be with his Heavenly Father following a brief illness. Born in Johnston County, he was the youngest of ten children born to Roby and Elizabeth Evans McKeel. Richard was a graduate of Princeton High School and Carolina Bible Institute and also served his country in the US Army during the Vietnam War. He has been a Free Will Baptist Minister since 1992, the last 15 years at Stevens Chapel Original Free Will Baptist Church near Benson. Richard was a devoted husband and Christian as well as a loving father and grandfather.

Rev Bushrod Washington Nash, Sr
Birth
24 Mar 1831
Westmoreland County, Virginia
Death
26 Jan 1911
Goldsboro, Wayne County, North Carolina
Burial
Willow Dale Cemetery
Goldsboro, Wayne County, North Carolina

Son of James R. Nash (~1788-?) and Martha Washington (~1800-?) both of Westmoreland County, Virginia. He served as a Baptist minister.

Rev Walter Brown Nobles
Birth:
May 3, 1866
Pitt County, North Carolina

Death:
Jul. 8, 1960
Greenville
Pitt County, North Carolina
Burial:
Winterville Cemetery
Winterville
Pitt County, North Carolina
In list of NC minister's name in 1950.

Elder Isaac H Pipkin
Birth:
Feb. 28, 1835
Death:
Aug. 4, 1917
Burial:
Core Point Free Will Baptist Church Cemetery
Core Point
Beaufort County, North Carolina

A minister in the early work of Free Will Baptists in North Carolina.
Inscription:
"I have fought a good fight, I have finished my course, I have kept the faith."

Addie H Outlaw
Birth:
Aug. 15, 1871
Death:
Nov. 27, 1942
Burial:
Suncrest Cemetery,
Monroe,
Union County,
North Carolina

Clarence H Overman, Jr
Birth:
Oct. 31, 1930
Death:
May 23, 2012
Pikeville, Wayne County,

North Carolina
Burial:
Pikeville Cemetery Pikeville,
Wayne County, North Carolina

At the age of fourteen, C.H. joined Union Grove Free Will Baptist Church, where his lifelong career with the Free Will Baptist denomination began. In 1952, he was ordained into the ministry and spent sixty years serving as a Free Will Baptist minister.

He graduated from Atlantic Christian College in 1957 with a degree in Religion and has held numerous pastorates in eastern North Carolina. The Rev. Overman was most recently a member of Rose Hill OFWB Church. C.H. also taught in the public-school system for 20 years and was a member of the Ayden Rotary Club for 31 years. Throughout the years he has served as pastor of 12 churches and served on various boards and committees. He served as editor of FWB press for more the 16 years, and general secretary of the OFWB Convention for more than five years.

Elder Henry Parker
Birth:
Sep. 28, 1840
Death:
Nov. 14, 1887
Burial:
Gum Swamp Freewill Baptist
Church Cemetery
Greenville
Pitt County
North Carolina

Wondering if he was descendant of Eld. Wm. Parker or Eld. Joseph Parker, early FWB ministers in this area? No grave maker found by contributor

Joseph Parker
Birth:
1711
Death:
1798
Burial:
Parker Family Cemetery
Windsor
Bertie County
North Carolina

Son of James Parker. Brother of Rueben. Probably kin the early Rev.

Joseph Parker, FWB preacher of that time.

Joseph Parker
Birth:
1705
Death:
1791 Wheat Swamp, Lenoir
County,
North Carolina
Burial:
Private burial ground on Cajah Barfied place,
Lenoir County,
North Carolina

He was one of the earliest founders and preachers in the Free Will Baptists is North Carolina. The Historical Commission of the North Carolina Original Free Will Baptist erected a highway sign there in 1966.

Today is not a day of demotion, But a day of crowning.

The marker in at the church started by Joseph Parker at about 1760 and remained a Free Will Baptist Church until 1843 when it was lost to the Disciples of Christ.

Joseph Parker is buried on a private plot near this church.

Rev Bryant Hanley Pate
Birth:
Oct. 17, 1879
Wake County, North Carolina
Death:
Jun. 27, 1959
Raleigh
Wake County, North Carolina
Burial:
Montlawn Memorial Park
Raleigh
Wake County, North Carolina

Rev. B.H. Pate was a minister in the Free Will Baptist Church, where his name is enumerated in a list of ordained ministers of the Free Will Baptist Western Conference Minutes held in Johnson Co., 1916. In the proceedings, Rev. B.H. Pate was elected financial officer of the Seminary for the Conference. Married his wife Hettie in Wilson County, NC. He was the son of Rev. Thomas J.D. Pate and Anna Hollard.

Inscription:
TOGETHER FOREVER

Rev Thomas JD Pate
Birth:
Aug. 13, 1848
Death:
1903
Burial:
Apex Cemetery
Apex
Wake County
North Carolina

Thomas Jefferson Pate was the son of Bryant Handley Pate and his wife Zilphia. He was pastor of Rock Springs Freewill Baptist Church on Olive Chapel Road at the crossroads near the Ed Clark homeplace near Apex, North Carolina. [He married Susan Ann HOLLAND, 17 August 1864]. He is brother to Zilphia Pate who married second Enos J. Holland.
--- from Holland Family Genealogy.

Rev Alexander "Alex" Paul
BIRTH
1841
Craven County, North Carolina,
USA
DEATH
24 Sep 1899 (aged 57–58)
New Bern, Craven County,
North Carolina, USA
BURIAL
Cedar Grove Cemetery
New Bern, Craven County,
North Carolina, USA

Christopher Lafayette Patrick
Birth:
Aug. 17, 1911
Death:
Dec. 9, 1996
Burial:
Snow Hill Cemetery,
Snow Hill, Greene County,
North Carolina

New Berne Weekly Journal, (New Bern, North Carolina) Friday, September 29, 1899, Page 3, Column 1. Rev. Alex Paul died Sunday night at his home in this city. The funeral was held yesterday afternoon at the Freewill Baptist church. He was a Confederate veteran** and many of the old comrades were present at the grave. His Enlistment Date: 1 Jan 1863 and his Rank at enlistment: Musician. Enlistment Place: Pitt County, North Carolina.

Service Record: Enlisted in Company E, North Carolina 1st Infantry Battalion on 01 Jan 1863. Mustered out on 18 Jan 1864. Transferred to Company E, North Carolina 67th Infantry Regiment on 18 Jan 1864. Sources: North Carolina Troops 1861-65, A Roster

Rev Hiram Gooding Paul
Birth:
Jan. 5, 1816
Death:
Jul. 8, 1865
Burial:
Cedar Grove Cemetery
New Bern
Craven County
North Carolina

His name is in a list of ministers and Elders belonging to OFWB conference. Taken from Minutes of NC Original Free Will Baptist Gen'l Conference held at Kit Swamp Meeting House, Craven Co. NC on the 9, 10, and 11th of Nov, 1854.

Thomas E. Peden
Birth:
Sep. 13, 1832
Huntington Township,
Gallia County, Ohio
Death:
Feb. 3, 1913
Ayden, Pitt County,
North Carolina
Burial:
Ayden Cemetery,
Ayden, Pitt County,
North Carolina

Ordained Free Will Baptist minister, church planter, college president and a faithful man to his calling. He was ordained May 8, 1859 in Syracuse, Meigs Co. OH, by Elders G. Goler and Ira. Z. Haning. He was still in college at the time but was teaching school and preaching to a congregation in the vicinity of Syracuse. He enlisted in Co. I, Ohio 173rd Infantry,16 Sep 1864 and mustered out 26 Jun 1865, at Nashville, TN (Official Records of the State of Ohio). He was active in the Ohio Yearly meeting and pastored The Harrisburg Free Will Baptist Church. He served as Associate pastor of Rio Grande Church, Ohio, while connected with the Rio Grande College faculty during the 1870/1880's. He also served on the council when the Gilboa FWB Church Ohio, was organized. He was aware that Free Will Baptists in the north were taking steps toward a union with another denomination, and that there were FWB churches in the South not affiliated with the northern churches, and he envisioned a possible union of these southern branches of FWB into a national organization. He announced through the "Free Will Baptist" that a Gen. Conf. would convene in Nashville, TN. Oct. 7, 1896. Subsequent meetings were held, and Dr. Peden was a leading advocate of this organization hoping to bring a union of North and South and avert any move toward a merger of the Northern FWB with another denomination. His dream was not realized but did succeed in drawing FWB in the South closer together. He was called from Ohio to the Seminary in Ayden, NC, beginning in 1899 (from his diary). He held the principalship until 1910, when he retired because of "age and declining health." Prof. Peden became head of the Theological Dept. when it was started. His tenure as head set the tone of the institution to provide a basic liberal arts education as well as theological training for a number of ministers who would render valuable services. He was well-liked, and esteemed by his peers, and honored for his service in the early beginning of the school. Rev. Robert F. Pittman, a graduate of the Seminary and a member of the faculty, conducted Prof. Peden's funeral.

Moses Washington Peterson
Birth:
Apr. 14, 1794
North Carolina
Death:
Aug. 1, 1879
Burial:
Peterson Hill Cemetery,
Burnsville,
Yancey County,
North Carolina

A spiritual leader and guide in an early time in our history serving mainly in Western North Carolina.

Edgar T. Phillips
Birth:
Mar. 26, 1857
North Carolina
Death:
Dec. 27, 1945
North Carolina
Burial:
Ayden Cemetery,
Ayden, Pitt County,North Carolina

Parents were Ray and Nancy (Jones) Phillips. He married Anna Hines, 23 Dec. 1891, in Wayne Co. NC (NC mar records).
In old Western Conf. minutes of 1916, convening in Johnston Co. NC, he was elected Secretary for the conference. He was also in the Minutes of Eastern Gen. Associational Minutes in the 1937 sessions and most likely others. Name in list of ordained ministers in N.C. living at Ayden.

Cedric Dixon Pierce, Jr
Birth:
Unknown
Wayne County, North Carolina
Death:
Oct. 23, 2012
Greenville
Pitt County, North Carolina
Burial:

Wayne Memorial Park
Goldsboro, Wayne County,
North Carolina

Pauline Pinyan
Birth:
unknown
Death:
Apr. 27, 2010
Kernersville, Forsyth County
North Carolina
Burial:
Eastlawn Gardens of Memory,
Kernersville,
Forsyth County, North Carolina

She was an ordained minister of the North Carolina State Association.

Elder Isaac H Pipkin
Birth:
Feb. 28, 1835
Death:
Aug. 4, 1917
Burial:
Core Point Free Will Baptist
Church Cemetery
Core Point
Beaufort County
North Carolina

Robert F. Pittman
Birth:
Nov. 8, 1883
Jerome, Bladen County,
North Carolina
Death
Jul. 15, 1938
Ayden,
Pitt County, North Carolina
Burial:
Ayden Cemetery,
Ayden,
Pitt County, North Carolina

An ordained Free Will Baptist minister and educator. He taught at Mt. Olive College, NC. He also pastored churches at Sweetgum Grove, Bethany, and Ayden, which erected an imposing stone at his death showing their admiration and esteem for his work among them.

Matthew C. Prescott
Birth:
1873
Death:
1943
Pamlico County, North Carolina
Burial:
Sand Hill Cemetery
Reelsboro, Pamlico County
North Carolina

Free Will Baptist minister in eastern North Carolina.

Francis Radford
Birth:
December 1, 1929,
Davidson County, North Carolina
Death:
Dec. 1, 2009
North Carolina
Burial:
Radford Cemetery
Madison County, North Carolina

Frances was valedictorian of her graduating class at Beech Glen High School when she was 16 years old in 1941. When Frances was a young girl, she went to a secret prayer place beneath a limb of an old fallen chestnut tree and fully surrendered her life to God. This full surrender meant giving up the plans to become a lawyer, and when she was 17 years old she became the first lady licensed to preach the gospel in the Free Will Baptist Churches in her area. Frances had a unique way of preaching the gospel by reaching the heights, depths and sweetness using illustrations in a way that made it a vivid, memorable message. Something you never forgot. It was so plain that the young could understand and so intense that the old were impressed and motivated. During her 60 plus years of active ministry, she served as pastor of several different churches in North Carolina and Tennessee and held revivals in many parts of the United States and Mexico. She was a member of Terry's Fork Free Will Baptist.

William Burkette Raper
Birth:
Sep. 10, 1927
Black Creek
Wilson County, North Carolina
Death:
Aug. 1, 2011
Mount Olive
Wayne County, North Carolina
Burial:
Friendship Free Will Baptist
Church Cemetery
Jones County, North Carolina

After the death of his father in 1936, Burkette entered the Free Will Baptist orphanage in Middlesex, North Carolina, where he lived until graduation from Middlesex High School in 1944.

He entered the ministry in the Free Will Baptist denomination in 1946 and was ordained by the Western Conference in North Carolina. He served as the pastor of the Oak Grove, Stony Hill, Memorial Chapel of the Free Will Baptist Children's Home in Nash County; Arapahoe in Pamlico County, Friendship in Jones County, Howell Swamp and Hull Road in Greene County. All were in North Carolina. He earned a Bachelor of Arts in Liberal Arts in 1947 from Duke University and a Master of Divinity in 1952 from the Duke Divinity School. He served as the Promotional Director of the Original Free Will Baptist State Convention between 1953 and 1954. On August 2, 1954 he became the president of Mount Olive College, Mount Olive, North Carolina while it was still a two year liberal arts college. At that time he was only age 26, which was the youngest college president in the United States and when he retired as president in January of 1995 he held the distinction of being the current longest tenured president in the nation. During his 40 years as president he guided the development of the college from a two-year junior college to an accredited four-year senior college. In 1960 Atlantic Christian College awarded him an honorary Doctor of Laws degree. In 1962, he earned a Master of Science in Higher Education from Florida State University. After retirement he served as the college's Director of Planned Giving for 10 years, making his tenure at the college a total of 50 years of service. Prior to his death, he held the distinction of being the longest tenured living ordained minister in the North Carolina Original FWB convention. Altogether, his ministry to his denomination led him to complete 65 years of service to God and mankind.

Archie W. Ratliff
Birth:
Nov. 29, 1949
Sneedville,
Hancock County, Tennessee
Death:
Dec. 17, 2012
Houston, Harris County, Texas
Burial:
Pinelawn Memorial Park,
Kinston,
Lenoir County, North Carolina

Senior Pastor of Bethel Free Will Baptist Church and Bethel Christian Academy in Kinston, NC, passed away at M.D. Anderson Cancer Center in Houston, Texas. Following graduation from Free Will Baptist Bible College in Nashville, Tn. Ratliff was ordained in 1972 in Glennville, Georgia, where he served five years as pastor of Glennville Free Will Baptist Church. He served as Moderator of the South Georgia Association from 1974 – 1976. and then Peace Free Will Baptist Church, Indianapolis, IN. He served as Moderator of the Indiana State Association for seven of his 14-year tenure there. Archie served as Senior Pastor of Bethel Free Will Baptist Church twenty-two years. Pastor Ratliff battled and defeated esophageal cancer in 2009; however, the radiation and chemotherapy treatments caused him to develop leukemia. Pastor Ratliff was a great respected leader in the Free Will Baptist Denomination. He served 12 years (1996 – 2008) on the Welch College Board of Trustees, including several years as vice chairman. And was very involved with Free Will Baptist International Missions. Pastor Ratliff guided Bethel Church to be globally involved in spreading the Gospel.

Willie E Renfrow
Birth:
Sep. 11, 1914
North Carolina
Death:
Oct. 23, 1970
North Carolina
Burial:
Branch Chapel Free Will Baptist
Church
Smithfield
Johnston County,
North Carolina

Rev. Willie E. and Sallie Hare Renfrow set up a Renfrow Family Endowment Scholarship for the Christian Ministry.

William Walter Reynolds
Birth:
Oct. 25, 1926
Columbia, Tyrrell County,
North Carolina
Death:
Dec. 22, 2009
Greenville,
Pitt County, North Carolina
Burial:
Hollywood Cemetery,
Farmville, Pitt County
North Carolina

A veteran of WWII (United States Army), he was ordained to the ministry of the Original Free Will Baptists (Albermarle Conference) on July 30, 1949. He graduated from Free Will Baptist Bible College in Nashville, TN, in 1951. He pastored churches in Tennessee and in North Carolina retiring in 2001.

Rev Ted Rondell Reynolds
BIRTH
3 Mar 1943
Haywood County, North Carolina,
USA
DEATH
2 Feb 2018 (aged 74)
Asheville, Buncombe County,
North Carolina, USA
BURIAL
Crawford-Ray Memorial Gardens
Clyde, Haywood County, North
Carolina, USA

Pastor Ted Rondell Reynolds, age 74, passed away at CarePartners Solace Center in Asheville.

A native of Haywood County, he was the son of the late Jess James Reynolds and Ella Mae Summey Reynolds. Pastor Ted was a member of Pisgah Freewill Baptist Church and had served as pastor for a number of churches for over 50 years. Funeral services in the Canton Chapel of Wells Funeral Home with the Pastor Jake Cagle and Reverend Elisha Fish officiating.

Mary Ellen Rice
Birth:
Unknown
Death:
Nov. 20, 2015
Morehead City
Carteret County
North Carolina
Burial: [Edit]
Bayview Cemetery
Morehead City
Carteret County
North Carolina

Mary Ellen Rice served for over 30 years at Beaufort Christian Academy, both as teacher and principal. Before that, she worked with the Child Evangelist Fellowship. She was also her church's first foreign missionary who served in Brazil on the field for seven years. She was always a godly lady and active in her church where she taught her junior class until her illness.

She is survived by her nieces and nephews and their families; Karen Hutton, Rhonda Sullivan, Roy F. Rice Jr., Jennifer Styron, John Rice, Greg Rice, Ruth D. Simpson, Leisha Mace, Kelly Sharpe, John Sharpe, Sandra Green, Janet Confer, Albert McElmon Jr. and R. L Rice; two sisters-in- law, Hyacinth Rice and Barabara "Bobbi- Ann" Rice Goodwin; her companion, Brancie Steele; and friends, Sarah Steele, Yvonne Humphrey and Douglas Elliott. Lastly, she is survived by the love of her life, Jon A. Swecker, her godson.

She was preceded in death by her

parents, Bonnie McCoy Rice and Sarah B. Rice; three brothers, Roy Fields Rice, Robert "Mousey" Rice and Gregory Rice; two sisters, Marie McElmon and Burnette Sharpe; two brothers-in-law, Joe Sharpe and Al McElmon; and two nephews, Danny Rice and Joseph Sharpe.

Her funeral service was held at the First Free Will Baptist Church in Morehead City with the Rev. Jerry Johnson officiating.

Gabriel Pinkney Rice
Birth:
Aug. 10, 1854
Marshall, North Carolina
Death:
Jan. 20, 1923
Asheville
Buncombe County,
North Carolina
Burial:
West Memorial Park
Weaverville
Buncombe County,
North Carolina

He was converted in 1875 and received his ordination on December 14, 1878. His ministry was in the vicinity of Eastern Tennessee, much of it having been spent in evangelistic work; he baptized about 1100 converts. He was the son of Isaac   Rachel Elizabeth Arrowroot Rice .

Roy Lee Rikard, Sr
Birth:
May 27, 1909
Caldwell County,
North Carolina
Death:
Mar. 14, 2008
Gastonia, Gaston County,
North Carolina
Burial:
Gaston Memorial Park,
Gastonia,
Gaston County, North Carolina

He was founder of Cramerton Free Will Baptist Church and a Bible Institute.

Fred A. Rivenbark, Sr
Birth:
Unknown
Duplin County, North Carolina
Death:
Aug. 23, 2000
Durham,
Durham County,
North Carolina
Burial:
Woodlawn Memorial Park,
Durham,
Durham County, North Carolina

He was a resident of Durham for 52 years. Rev. Rivenbark was born in Duplin County, N.C., and was a native of Mount Olive. The Rev. Rivenbark pastored Sherron Acres Free Will Baptist Church, prior to retiring from full-time ministry, and served on staff there as assistant pastor for 25 years. He also pastored Oak Grove Free Will Baptist Church in Durham, St. Paul Free Will Baptist Church, Elizabeth City, N.C., First Free Will Baptist Church, Wilson, N.C., Fairmont Park Free Will Baptist Church, Norfolk, Virginia Beach Free Will Baptist Church, and Stoney Creek Free Will Baptist Church, Goldsboro. In addition to pastoring seven churches, Mr. Rivenbark preached in hundreds of revival meetings.

Moses Duckworth Roberts
Birth:
May 13, 1869
Madison County
North Carolina, USA
Death:
Apr. 4, 1949
Buncombe County
North Carolina
Burial:
Union Chapel Church Cemetery
Weaverville
Buncombe County
North Carolina

An ordained Original Free Will Baptist minister, whose death was noted in the Minutes of the Western Conference, the next session after his death.
Son of John Roberts and Mary Reece

Rev John Alfred Rouse
Birth:
Jan. 31, 1861
Duplin County
North Carolina
Death:
Mar. 7, 1947
Wilmington
New Hanover County
North Carolina
Burial:
Clay Hill Cemetery
Rose Hill
Duplin County, North Carolina

Listed in 1903 Cape Fear Conference, meeting at Hodges Chapel church, Harnett Co. NC.

Oscar Patrick "Pate" Rose
Birth:
Aug. 2, 1860
Johnston County
North Carolina
Death:
Feb. 27, 1938
Selma
Johnston County
North Carolina
Burial:
Snipes-Pearce Cemetery
Princeton
Johnston County
North Carolina

Rev. O.P. Rose was an ordained minister serving in Johnson and surrounding counties. His name is listed in the roll of ministers in the 35th session of the Western Conference, meeting at Holly Springs, Johnson Co., Oct. 13, 1921.

Rev Joseph Kindred Ruffin
Birth:
Apr. 29, 1861
Death:
Feb. 5, 1939
Burial:
Rock Springs Free Will Baptist Church Cemetery
Bailey
Nash County
North Carolina

Name in list of ordained Free Will Bapt. ministers, 1935 Association minutes. Son of John Davis Ruffin and Mary Ann Mercer.

Cross Creek Cemetery #1
Fayetteville
Cumberland County
North Carolina,

Rev. Joseph Salmon's name is in a list of 1903 ministers of the E. Conf. meeting in Harnett Co., at Hodges Chapel Church, NC. Also, there are marriages in county performed by, Rev. Joseph Salmon, Bapt. minister.
Company B, 36th North Carolina Infantry, Confederate States Of America.

John Ephriam Sawyer
Birth:
Jan. 26, 1886
Death:
May 15, 1962
Arlington, Virginia
Burial:
Ayden Cemetery, Ayden,
Pitt County, North Carolina

Rev Joseph Salmon
Birth:
1842
Death:
Mar. 23, 1914
Burial:

He studied at Ayden Seminary after which he received his ministerial credentials. Later, he was principal at Ayden Seminary and taught at the Seminary for eight years until he was 76 years of age. He believed in a strong academic program coupled with a strong biblical foundation. He was a fluent speaker who took the ministry seriously.

William Riley Sawyer
Birth:
Jul. 20, 1884
Merritt, Pamlico County,
North Carolina
Death:
Oct. 17, 1922
Pamlico County, North Carolina
Burial:
Trent Free Will Baptist Church
Cemetery
Pamlico County, North Carolina

He was affiliated most of his life with the Trenton Free Will Baptist Church, Merritt, Pamlico County North Carolina. He was associated with the Free Will Baptist Press as early as 1874 as an agent, and was on the Board of Directors from at least 1895 until 1900. He became president of the company in 1901 and continued until 1912. He was the father of John E. Sawyer.

John Clinton Simpson
BIRTH
11 Mar 1940
Verona, Boone County, Kentucky
DEATH
16 Mar 2019
Winterville, Pitt County, North
Carolina
BURIAL
Pinewood Memorial Park
Greenville, Pitt County,
North Carolina

He graduated from Williamsburg High School in Williamsburg, Ohio in 1958 and married his high school sweetheart, Barbara Joy, in 1959.

Their marriage was blessed by 4 children; Johnny, Jerry, Angela and Timothy.

John graduated from Cincinnati Bible Seminary in 1972 and entered full time ministry. He pastored churches in Kentucky, Ohio, Virginia and North Carolina. Most recently he pastored at Bethany FWB Church in Winterville and then attended upon retiring. Most of all, John had a great love for God, his family and for people. He had a great sense of humor and always liked to tell a joke. He had a beautiful bass voice and loved to sing in church. He sang in the choir, sang solos and often sang with his wife, Barbara.

Rev David Robert Stafford
Birth:
Jan. 11, 1844
Death:
Sep. 27, 1914
Burial:
Antioch United Methodist Church
Cemetery
Strickland Crossroads
Johnston County
North Carolina

His name appears in roll of ministers in 1903 Minutes of the Free Will Baptist church, when it convened at Hodges Chapel church, Harnett Co. NC. He also was enlisted in the CSA NC 20th Reg. Co. H; entered Pvt, Final rank: Sgt.

Rev Spartan D Scalf
Birth:
Oct. 10, 1862
Greenville, Greenville County
South Carolina
Death:
Aug. 24, 1920
Durham, Durham County
North Carolina
Burial:
Maplewood Cemetery
Durham, Durham County
North Carolina

Eld. S.D. Scalf, age 60 years of the Eastern Conference, spirit took its flight from earth to glory, Aug. 24, 1920. He was a resident of Durham, NC. And a member of Mineral Springs Free Will Baptist Church. He was a pious, good and faithful member as well as a preacher. Son of Henry & Rebecca Jones Scalf. He died of paralysis living only 22 hrs. from onset. The funeral was preached by Rev. T. C. Marks in the presence of a large crowd, after which this body was placed in the Durham Cemetery to await the resurrection.

Rev Carlee Elizabeth Smith Stallard
Birth:
Nov. 20, 1927
Wise County
Virginia
Death:
Unknown
Burial:
Mount Gur Cemetery
Kernersville
Forsyth County
North Carolina

Her name is in the Original Free Will Baptist Directory of Ordained NC Ministers, showing she was a member of Piedmont Conference, and serving Piedmont Church House of Prayer. Wife of Lee Hardrick Stallard, 1920-1986.

Adam Scott
Birth:
Jan. 23, 1917
Texas County, Missouri
Death:
Mar. 26, 2004
North Carolina
Burial:
Knollwood Cemetery, Clayton, Johnston County, North Carolina

He was a Free Will Baptist minister and part of a large relationship consisting of ministers with names of Scott, Smith, and Vandivort that had ministries across the FWB denomination.

Rev Gordon R. Sebastian

BIRTH
22 Mar 1936
DEATH
22 Mar 2018
BURIAL
Evergreen Memorial Park
Wilson, Wilson County,
North Carolina

Rev. Gordon R. Sebastian, 86 of Wilson passed away Thursday and his funeral services will be conducted at Peace Church and the Reverent Rusty Russell will officiate. A graveside service with Military Honors was held . Rev. Sebastian pastored for over fifty-three years, including forty years at Peace Church. He served his country honorable and faithfully with the U.S. Navy. An ordained Free Will Baptist minister who was active in all levels of his denomination and was once a speaker at the national convention before thousands of attendees. He was a WW II Navy Veteran, who served both God and country honorably.

Rev Ervin Daniel Sluder

Birth:
Oct. 22, 1887
Buncombe County
North Carolina, USA
Death:
Apr. 18, 1970
Weaverville
Buncombe County
North Carolina
Burial:

Mountain View FW Baptist Church
Cemetery
Leicester
Buncombe County
North Carolina

Parents: John Sluder (1845 - 1915) - Malinda Minerva Black Sluder (1852 - 1938), Spouse:Hester DeWeese Sluder (1888 - 1961).

Samra Smith

Birth:
Jul. 31, 1891
Death:
Nov. 25, 1923
North Carolina, USA
Burial:
Mount Olive Baptist Church
Cemetery
Mount Olive
Stokes County, North Carolina

Rev. Samra Smith (a North Carolina native) had merged his publication, the Biblical Beacon, into the New Morning Star published by S. L. Morris of Texas and whose publication was representing the Co-operative General Association with the news of the new movement. He became one of the early presidents of Tecumseh College and pastor of the Tecumseh Church. Smith also taught Chemistry and Biology at the college and his wife Pearl Smith taught Preparatory Work. He served as Moderator of the Co-operative General Association

LTC David Leonard Spears
Birth:
Nov. 24, 1960
Vicenza,Veneto, Italy
Death:
Dec. 25, 2011
Sanford, Lee County,
North Carolina
Burial:
Jonesboro Cemetery,
Sanford, Lee County,
North Carolina

Free Will Baptist minister and Chaplain. Chaplain (LTC) David Leonard Spears, 51, of Sanford, died at his residence.

David was a member of the Kendale Acres Free Will Baptist Church.

The funeral at Kendale Acres Free Will Baptist Church with Rev. Richard Barnes and CH (CPT) Ken Lewis officiating.

R. B. Spencer
Birth:
Mar. 2, 1886
Pamlico County,
North Carolina
Death:
Jan. 25, 1954
Pitt County, North Carolina
Burial:
Ayden Cemetery, Ayden,
Pitt County, North Carolina

A minister and educator. He was educated in Whitsett Institute and the University of North Carolina. He taught for a number of years. In 1932 he was ordained to the gospel Ministry. He was elected to the position of Editor of "The Free Will Baptist" in 1936, which position he held until September 1953. He was a member of Little Creek Free Will Baptist Church. Funeral services were held at the Free Will Baptist Church by the Rev. R. N. Hinnant, of Micro, assisted by the Rev. Bruce Barrow of Snow Hill, and the Rev. Charles Craddock of Ayden.

Rev David Robert Stafford
Birth:
Jan. 11, 1844
Death:
Sep. 27, 1914
Burial:
Antioch United Methodist Church
Cemetery
Strickland Crossroads
Johnston County
North Carolina

His name appears in roll of ministers in 1903 Minutes of the Free Will Baptist church, when it convened at Hodges Chapel church, Harnett Co. NC. He also was enlisted in the CSA NC 20th Reg. Co. H; entered Pvt, Final rank: Sgt.

Rev Carlee Elizabeth Smith Stallard
BIRTH
20 Nov 1927
Wise County, Virginia, USA
DEATH
unknown
BURIAL
Mount Gur Cemetery
Kernersville, Forsyth County,
North Carolina, USA

Wife of Lee Hardrick Stallard, 1920-1986.

Her name is in the Original FreeWill Baptist Directory of Ordained NC Ministers, showing she was a member of Piedmont Conference, and serving Piedmont Church House of Prayer

Rev Thomas Walter Stancil
Birth:
Jul. 3, 1880
Wilson, North Carolina
Death:
Jul. 14, 1959
Woodard Herring Hospital
Wilson, Wilson Co., NC
Burial:
Piney Grove Church Cemetery
Nash County
North Carolina

An ordained Free Will Baptist minister in the Western Conference of FWB, listed in 1916 conference minutes.

Chester V. Stanley
Birth:
1912
North Carolina
Death:
1968
North Carolina
Burial:

Bethel Original Freewill Baptist Church Cemetery, Four Oaks, Johnston County, North Carolina

James Dallas Stepps
Birth:
Nov. 2, 1940
Pitt County, North Carolina
Death:
Sep. 2, 2013
Duffield
Scott County, Virginia
Burial:
Pinewood Memorial Park
Greenville
Pitt County, North Carolina,

Rev. James "Dallas" Stepps, 72, a native of Pitt County, was a graduate of Hookerton High School and attended FWB Bible College in Nashville, TN. He pastored in TN, SC, NC and in FL for 30 years, and for 15 years served as the NC Advancement Representative for Harvest FWB Child Care Ministries in Duffield, VA. He was a member of Unity FWB Church.

Rev James Lawrence Strickland
Birth:
Apr. 19, 1843
Death:
Dec. 5, 1929
Burial:
Flood Chapel FWB Church
Cemetery
Floods Chapel
Nash County, North Carolina

Rev. J.L. Strickland was an ordained Free Will Bapt. minister. James is the son of Hariett Strickland. He married Sallie C. Robinson, daughter of Joe and Edna Roberson.
U.S. Civil War Enlisted in Company A, North Carolina 47th Infantry Regiment on 11 Apr 1862. Mustered out on 09 Apr 1865 at Appomattox Court House, VA.

Simon Hill Styron, Jr
Birth:
Mar., 1891
Sealevel
Carteret County, North Carolina
Death:
Dec. 17, 1939
Pine Level, Johnston County,
North Carolina
Burial:
Oliver Cemetery
Johnston County, North Carolina

Early Free Will Baptist minister serving in North Carolina. He was married to Ida Oliver. His parents were Simon Hill Styron (1851 - 1933) Nancy Lupton Styron and his son was Simon Daniel Styron (1925 - 1990).

Thomas O. Terry, Jr
Birth:
1921
Death:
2009
Craven County,
North Carolina
Burial:
Greenleaf Memorial Park,
New Bern,
Craven County
North Carolina

He was a Free Will Baptist minister in eastern North Carolina.

Rev John Samuel Thompson
Birth:
Jul. 25, 1860
Death:
Dec. 11, 1938
Burial:
Woodlawn Memorial Park
Durham
Durham County
North Carolina

Listed in roll of Free Will Bapt. ordained ministers in Minutes of 49th Session of Western Conference, which convened in 1935, and then his death reported as the year before in the 1939th Session. He was active minister/pastor and serving until his death.

Rev Duffy Toler
Birth:
Oct. 4, 1881
Death:
Sep. 6, 1955
Burial:
Oakdale Cemetery
Washington
Beaufort County
North Carolina

An active ordained minister in the Free Will Baptist church. His name appears in many old church records, serving on boards, committees, and as pastor

Dr William F. Toler
Birth:
Jun. 26, 1946
Death:
May 9, 2017
Dunn Crossroads
Wilson County
North Carolina
Burial:
Elmwood
Fremont
Wayne County,North Carolina

Reverend Dr. William F. "Billy" Toler, 70, Free Will Baptist minister, of Elm City and services was at the First Free Will Baptist Church, Wilson. Surviving is his wife of 51 years, Margie Proctor Toler; son, Lee Toler of Pikeville; daughter, Cindy Toler (Danny Miller) of Cape Carteret; special grandson, Ashton Toler, Devin Murray and their mother, Susan

Murray; granddaughters, Morgan and Madison Miller; sisters, Jean Summerlin of Macclesfield and Rachel Ruffin of Whitakers; mother-in-law, Isabell Proctor of Fremont; sisters-in-law, Shirley (Ricky) Winders, Sue Proctor, Connie (Richard) Kidd, brothers-in-law, Larry (Brenda) Proctor of Fremont and Mike Proctor of Cedar Point; a host of nieces and nephews as well as very special friends.

He served God for over 35 years and touched many lives and loved every minute of it - never feeling that he sacrificed anything. He went from being a sharecropper's son to having more riches and blessings than any one person could ever imagine. His Favorite verse: In the Beginning God (Genesis 1:1).

And with unfaltering lip and heart, I call the Saviour mine.

Herbert Turner Tripp
Birth:
Sep. 2, 1909
Death:
Oct. 17, 1981
Burial:
Juniper Chapel FWB Church Cemetery
Vanceboro
Craven County
North Carolina

Listed with names of organizers of NC State Association of FWB, from Vanceboro.

Inscription:
Gone to be with his Lord
Granddaddy Herbert

Rev Benjamin Wesley Tippett
Birth:
Feb. 15, 1856
Johnston, North Carolina
Death:
May 8, 1922
Little River;Zehulsa, Wake
Burial:
Harris Daniel Cemetery
Middlesex, Nash County
North Carolina

Rev. B.B. Tippett, was an ordained minister in the Original Free Will Baptist church and was active in the Western Conference of Free Will Baptist churches. His name is among ordained ministers in the Thirteenth session Minutes for said conference, held in 1916, and in earlier church records. Besides as pastor of churches, he held positions on boards and committees in the Conference and lived a useful life.

Benjamin is the son of William Tippett and Elizabeth Hinton. He married Mary Jane Daniel, daughter of Harris Daniel and Mourning Jane Tisdale about 1879.

Elder James Turnage
BIRTH
10 Jun 1821
DEATH
2 Nov 1882 (aged 61)
BURIAL
Hodges Chapel Cemetery
Benson, Johnston County,
North Carolina

A Free Will Baptist minister, listed as being one of the original ministers of churches from 1855-1901, in Cape Fear Conference. He was married to Sarah E. Turnage whose lifespan follows 1834–1894.

Archibald Alfred. Tyson
Birth:
Nov. 28, 1838
Death:
Apr. 27, 1914
Burial:
Pineview Cemetery
South Rocky Mount
Edgecombe County,
North Carolina

This info is from a 1937 cemetery survey compiled by the Historical Records Survey of North Carolina and located in the Family Records Collection of the State Archives. It appears here exactly as written in that document.

Rev Marvin Earl "Jack" Tyson
Birth:
Mar. 4, 1901
Greene County
North Carolina
Death:
Oct. 10, 1953
Carrboro
Orange County
North Carolina
Burial:
Hollywood Cemetery
Farmville
Pitt County
North Carolina

Son of Willie Tyson and Pattie Worthington Tyson. Married to Stella Irene Hart around 1920. An ordained Free Will Baptist minister and shown as such in 1935 NC Minutes. Superintendent Free Will Baptist Orphanage.
U.S. WWII Draft Cards Young Men, 1940-1947

Rev A. B. Utley
Birth:
Sep. 25, 1859
Death:
Oct. 8, 1938
Burial:
Collins Grove Baptist Church Cemetery
Holly Springs
Wake County
North Carolina

He was an ordained Free Will Bapt. minister, listed in the 1935 minutes of the Western Conference. He was an active minister and pastor.

Jacob Utley

Birth:
Nov. 6, 1803
Raleigh
Wake County, North Carolina
Death:
Mar. 28, 1888
Thomasville
Davidson County, North Carolina
Burial:
Gods Acre
Thomasville
Davidson County, North Carolina

Rev. Jacob Utley was an early pioneer Free Will Baptist minister in NC, whose name appears as one of the several ministers who helped sustain the scattered churches after 1832. On Sept. 1, 1887, he came to the orphanage as a home for aged ministers. No others were ever received as the plan was abandoned.

Spouse: Aplis Wallace Utley (1810 - 1888).

Inscription:
Native of Wake County, for many years a missionary pastor in North Carolina.

Elder Jesse Vause

Birth:
Dec., 1799
Death:
Jun. 29, 1854
Burial:
Vause Family Cemetery,
Lenoir County,
North Carolina

An early Free Will Baptist minister, named in a list of ministers who had been active in the old Bethel Conference, and declining to unite in a merger, but rather restricted consolidation with another group.

Rev Alonzo A. Wells

Birth:
Sep. 9, 1896
Death:
Jul. 1, 1939
Burial:
Raines Crossroads Cemetery
Princeton

Johnston County
North Carolina

An ordained Free Will Baptist minister, listed in the minutes of the 49th Session of the Western Conference, NC, convened in 1935.

Inscription:
Faithful to their trust even unto death

Robert West
Birth:
1947
Death:
2009
Burial:
Hills of Neuse Memorial Gardens, Smithfield, Johnston County, North Carolina

Free Will Baptist pastor and missionary to the Ivory Coast, Africa.

Pamela "Pam" Stanley West
Birth:
Feb. 7, 1949
Johnston County
North Carolina
Death:
Oct. 9, 2016
Four Oaks
Johnston County
North Carolina
Burial:
Hills of Neuse Memory Gardens
Smithfield
Johnston County
North Carolina

Pamela "Pam" S. West was born to the late Thomas Milford and Ada Pearl Hall Lassiter Stanley. She was a secretary with Rose & Graham Funeral Home in Four Oaks and the former Minshew Funeral Home. She and her husband served as missionaries to Ivory Coast West Africa for 21 years. She was a member of Unity Free Will Baptist Church in Smithfield.

Rev Luke Wetherington
Birth:
1890
Death:
1944
Burial:
Cedar Grove Cemetery
New Bern
Craven County
North Carolina

An ordained Free Will Baptist minister in Craven Co. Amazon sells a book of his life, "A Chosen Vessel-Luke Herbert Wetherington.

Lee Whaley
Birth:
1914
Death:
1988
North Carolina
Burial:
Pinelawn
Memorial Park,
Kinston, Lenoir County,
North Carolina

He was a Free Will Baptist pastor serving in various pastorates and was a home missionary to Alaska.

John Wheeler
Birth:
Jan. 1, 1800
North Carolina
Death:
Aug. 15, 1871
Yancey County, North Carolina
Burial:

Silvers Cemetery, Pensacola, Yancey County, North Carolina

He was a early minister and leader whose legacy spreads across a four state area consisting of N.C., TN., Va. West Va.

Elder Jonas Hardie Whitley
Birth:
Dec. 5, 1875
North Carolina
Death:
Jul. 7, 1941
North Carolina
Burial:
Rock Springs
Free Will Baptist
Church Cemetery
Bailey
Nash County
North Carolina

An ordained Free Will Bapt. minister, useful in service of his church.

Rev Phillip Carl Wiggs
Birth:
Oct. 29, 1907
Death:
Apr. 8, 1974
Burial:
Queen Anne Cemetery
Fountain
Pitt County
North Carolina,

Ordained Free Will Baptist minister whose name appears in church records and obits of funerals he has conducted.

I Am Come That You May Have Life Abundantly

Nestus VanDelon Wiggs
Birth:
Mar. 23, 1889
Pine Level, Johnson Co.,
N.C
Death:
Jan. 13, 1941
Burial:
Cedar Grove Cemetery,
New Bern, Craven County,
North Carolina

Theodore "Ted" Edwin Wilbanks
Birth:
May 10, 1940
Oklahoma
Death:
June 2, 2019
Garner, North Carolina
Burial:
Bethel Free Will Baptist church
Cemetery,
Four Oaks, North Carolina

He was a member of the Eastern Conference. In 1912 he entered the Free Will Baptists Seminary in Ayden for his Theological study while serving churches in the eastern part of N.C. He was active in revival work and other activities of the Denomination. He served as moderator of the Union Meeting and was a member of the Church Extension Board of the State Convention of N.C. for several years. His funeral was conducted by D.W. Alexander, J.L. Hodges and J.C. Griffin.

Rev. Wilbanks was born to the late William Edwin and Opal Lacefield Wilbanks. He was an ordained minister and pastor of music ministry.
Funeral services at C3 Church, Clayton. Officiating will be Pastor Matt Fry.

Daniel Anderson Windham
Birth:
Nov. 7, 1887
Wilson County
North Carolina
Death:
Jun. 17, 1961
Greenville
Pitt County
North Carolina
Burial:
Greenwood Cemetery
Greenville
Pitt County, North Carolina

A North Carolina minister who was the Son of William Edward Windham and Sarah Elizabeth (Rasberry) Windham.

Missionary
Emma Ruth *Bennett* Willey
Birth:
Dec. 19, 1935
Death:
Dec. 13, 1972
Panama City,
Panama, Panama
Burial:
New Bern Memorial Cemetery,
Trent Woods,
Craven County, North Carolina,
Plot: Section A

Served as a missionary in Panama for Free Will Baptist missions. She served as a missionary in the interior as well as the capital Panama City. She died in the Gorgus hospital in Panama City and was returned to New Bern for her burial. She was the wife of Thomas Willey, Junior.

Missionary
Zadie Volena Wilson
Birth:
Mar. 11, 1918
Rutherford County,
North Carolina
Death:
Mar. 30, 2001
McDowell County,
North Carolina
Burial:
McDowell Memorial Park,
Marion
McDowell County,
North Carolina

A missionary to India for many years. She later worked for the

Presbyterian Journal until her retirement. During her retirement, she continued to be faithful in ministry visiting the hospitals, nursing homes and shut-ins. She also continued to promote the missionary endeavor in India through her many speaking engagements in churches.

Rev Daniel Anderson Windham
BIRTH
7 Nov 1887
Wilson County, North Carolina,
DEATH
17 Jun 1961 (aged 73)
Greenville, Pitt County,
North Carolina
BURIAL
Greenwood Cemetery
Greenville, Pitt County,
North Carolina

A Free Will Baptist minister in Greenville area, and name listed in roll of ministers in the conference.

Marcellus A. Woodard
Birth:
September 6, 1879
Greene County, North Carolina
Death:
1957
Pitt County, North Carolina
Burial:
Reedy Branch Baptist Church,
Winterville,
Pitt County, North Carolina

An early Free Will Baptist preacher who in 1903 at the age of 24 was licensed to preach the gospel at Howell Swamp Free Will Baptist Church, Greene County, North Carolina. He prepared for the ministry at the Free Will Baptist Seminary, in Ayden and began his early ministry in the Midway Association in South Georgia in 1909. He married the daughter of W.A. McDonald, a pioneer Free Will Baptist minister in South Georgia. His ministry existed in South Georgia and North Florida until the fall of 1921, when he returned to his native state becoming the pastor of the church in Davis, North Carolina. For 53 years he was a faithful minister the gospel with 32 of those years as a member of the Central conference of North Carolina..

T. E. Woody
Birth:
Apr. 4, 1876
Death:
Dec. 10, 1967
Yancey County, North Carolina
Burial:
Will Young Cemetery,
Yancey County,North Carolina

A Free Will Baptist minister who was active in the organization of the N C State Association of Orig. FWB. Free Will Baptist preacher in western North Carolina.

Rev James William Wooten
Birth:
Jul. 2, 1922
Death:
Jan. 30, 1987
Burial:
Mount Harmony Baptist Church
Matthews
Mecklenburg County
North Carolina

Rev Joseph Ernest Wooten
Birth:
Jun. 4, 1888
North Carolina
Death:
Apr. 10, 1970
Burial:
Ayden Cemetery
Ayden
Pitt County
North Carolina

Rev. J. E. Wooten was a Free Will Baptist minister, pastor, teacher and leader. He moved from place to place to pastor but before 1940, he was in Ayden, where the FWB Press was located, publishing Sunday School literature and other materials for the denomination. He was writing Sunday School

Literature for them. He was an ordained Free Will Baptist minister in the Eastern General Association in 1930's; he was pastor and evangelist for many years, active in all the work.

He was married to Sudie TRIPP, 28 Sept. 1913, and they lived in several places probably due to his ministerial work serving at different churches. Sudie d. in 1927, and bur where his parents and other family members were in Greene Co.

Rev. J. E. married 2) Lucy Lenora Harris in 1928, and they made their home in Beaufort, Chocowinity (see 1930 census).

Lucy and J.E. had children:
James Russell Wooten, 1930 and Minnie Carol Wooten, in 1932.
Lucy died in 1944.

Sometime later he married Daisy (Adams) Davidson, a widow of a noted FWB minister who had died in 1938 an untimely death. She and Wooten had no children together.